# FRONTIER LEGACY

## History of the Olympic National Forest 1897 to 1960

# FRONTIER LEGACY

---

## History of the Olympic National Forest 1897 to 1960

---

J.R. Rooney

Frontier Legacy: History of the Olympic National Forest 1897 to 1960

by J.R. Rooney

Copyright © 1997, 2007
Northwest Interpretive Association

Published by
Northwest Interpretive Association
164 South Jackson Street, Seattle, WA 98104
www.nwpubliclands.org

ISBN-10: 0-914019-58-9
ISBN-13: 978-0-914019-58-9

Printed in the United States of America

All rights reserved. No part of this publication may be reproduced or transmitted in any form or by any means, electronic or mechanical, including photocopy, recording, digital reproduction, or any information storage and retrieval system, without permission in writing from the publisher.

Northwest Interpretive Association (NWIA) is a 501(c)(3) nonprofit corporation based in Seattle, Washington and licensed to operate in Oregon, Idaho, California, and Montana. For more than 30 years NWIA has provided resources to promote enhanced enjoyment and understanding of Northwest public lands. Through partnerships with the USDA Forest Service, National Park Service, US Army Corps of Engineers, Washington State Parks, City of Seattle Public Utilities, and Bureau of Reclamation NWIA acts as a crucial supporter of public lands, helping to educate visitors by providing valuable information about the lands we all share in common. For more information, please visit our website at **www.nwpubliclands.org**.

Book and Cover Design by Ben Nechanicky

*To the men and women of the Olympic, past and present...*

*and the people they serve.*

## Acknowledgements

The author would like to thank the following persons who were so gracious in sharing their personal memories of the past:

Mrs. Katherine Flaherty—daughter of Chris Morgenroth; Mrs. Rudo (Eleanor) Fromme; Mrs. Orlo (Iva) Higley; Mr. T. R. Rixon—Grandson of Theodore Rixon; Mr. John (Jack) Schwartz —Forest Service, retired

Fellow Authors:

Harriet Fish—who provided clues and historical facts & whose enthusiasm proved contagious; Ruby El Hult—for writing *Untamed Olympics* and for her unselfish encouragement and support; Del McBride—for his generosity and care; Eva Cook Taylor—who knew the forest trails and shared her love for the Olympics

Technical Support:

Diane Converse & Gail Saunders—graphic consultants; Julie Hiller—computer services; Ken Eldredge—photographic consultation; Donald L. Ray—office services

With special thanks to editor and colleague, T. I. "Dutch" Notenboom

# CONTENTS

*"The most remarkable mountain we had seen on the coast of New Albion, now presented itself. Its summit, covered with eternal snow, was divided into a very elegant double fork, and rose conspicuously from a base of lofty mountains clothed in the same manner, which descended gradually to hills of a moderate height, and terminated like that we had seen the preceding day, in low cliffs falling perpendicularly on a sandy beach; off which were scattered many rocks and rocky islets of various forms and sizes. This was generally considered, though it was not confirmed by its latitude, to be the mount Olympus of Mr. Meares; it being the only conspicuous mountain we had observed on the part of the coast we had visited. Mount Olympus is placed in latitude 47' 10'; whereas our latitude now was 47' 38'; and as this mountain bore N. 55 E., it must consequently be to the north of us; although we were unable to determine its precise situation, by the thick hazy weather which shortly succeeded. [sic]*

*Vancouver's Journals, Pages 41-42*

*Captain George Vancouver's HMS Discovery (From an 1890 Etching) Zig-zag Journeys in the Great Northwest, Hezekiah Butterworth*

*...By virtue of this, these lands belong to the said royal crown of Castille and Leon and as such he takes and took possession of these lands and the neighboring seas, rivers, ensenadas, ports, bays, gulfs, archipelagos, and this Bay of Nunez Gaona where at present, this vessel is anchored, and places them in subordination to and under the power, possession and domain of the royal crown of Castille and Leon...*

With these words, a wooden cross of possession was formally placed in the sand in 1790 by Captains from Castille sailing north from Mexico. Spain's claim to the territory of Alta California was made more secure with this new colony in a strange forbidding land of mountains, forests, and furs.

Previous contact with the natives had been made by Spanish vessels in 1775 when Bodega Y Quadra and Bruno Heceta landed at Port Grenville near the mouth of Quinault River. The longboat with seven people aboard had accidentally beached at a restricted site for native women; a tribal taboo had been violated; the longboat was seized, five occupants killed and two drowned while trying to escape. Prior accounts of Russians being shipwrecked and living with the Indians had been reported. The northern Spanish foothold was abandoned just two years after the wooden cross had been planted at Neah Bay. All Spanish claims on the northwest coast were relinquished forever with the sale of Florida in 1819. Meanwhile, American and English influence grew while the menace of Russian pelt hunters spread south from their stronghold in Alaska.

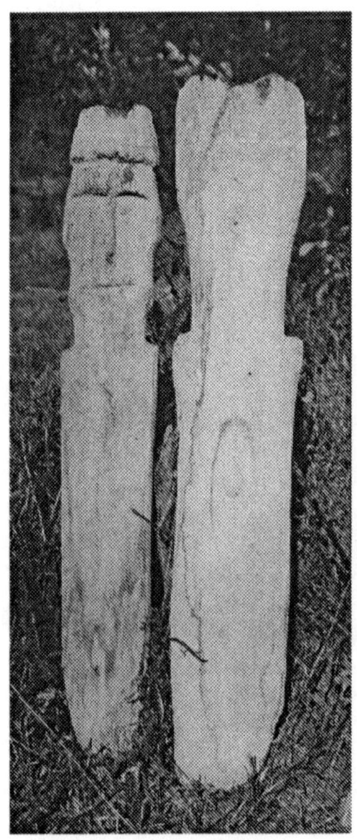

*House Posts representing Spirit Figures, Lake Cushman. Photo by Addison Ludden, date unknown*

Captain Vancouver's vessel, *Discovery*, was well named. The English admiralty ordered him to chart the northwest coast from 30 to 60 degrees north latitude. As they anchored at New Dungeness, a distant mountain was observed by Lieutenant Baker and now bears his name. Many other geographic features were named by Captain Vancouver and another trusted lieutenant, Peter Puget. The Russians and Spaniards had previously explored these waters in search of the fabled Northwest Passage, inspired by the legend of a feisty Greek pilot who sailed under the Spanish flag and the name, Juan de Fuca. Even the greatest navigator of his time, the famous Captain Cook, failed to find the fabled strait, having sailed north to Nootka Bay exchanging pieces of iron and beads for sea otter skins. This third voyage of Captain Cook resulted in the expansion of the maritime fur trade, but only at the expense of his own death by

Polynesians in Hawaii. Americans, called "Boston Men" by the natives, led by Captain Robert Gray, helped to dispel the myth of the Northwest Passage to the Atlantic.

Who were these first Americans on the Olympic Peninsula when the Europeans voyaged in search of riches and conquest? It is believed that their ancestors were nomadic hunters and gatherers who used primitive stone tools; they hunted the woolly mammoth, mastodon, bison and caribou which provided food and materials for clothing and other implements. After the continental glaciers retreated from the land, climate and vegetation changed; settlements were established on the beaches and these natives relied more on sea life for food. They used cedar to make houses, canoes, and clothing, and they gathered camas, fern roots and wild berries. Seasonal hunting and fishing camps were established inland up the river valleys. The migrating salmon, along with the bountiful shellfish, provided the staple foodstuff for these early Americans. At the point of historic contact, the Quinault, Quileute, and Makah were active whalers who, armed with bone and mussel shell-pointed harpoons hewed of sturdy yew wood, manned large canoes. They were the only tribes in North America to pursue these large mammals. The traditional life of the Northwest natives was altered forever by the conflict of cultures and introduction of social diseases.

*Quileute Man With House Post. Courtesy State Capitol Museum*

*Billy Mason, Son of Chief Taholah. Courtesy Del McBride*

*Chief Taholah With Wife. Courtesy Del McBride*

*...Steadily, the frontier of settlement advanced and carried with it individualism, democracy, and nationalism... In this advance, the frontier is the outer edge of the wave...*

*Frederick Jackson Turner, The Significance of The Frontier in American History*

Great Britain and its remaining rival, the United States, signed a joint occupation treaty of the Oregon Country which sealed the fate of the Indian Tribes, which were soon confined to reservations while their former lands were opened to settlement by fur trappers, traders, and miners. Jefferson County was created by the Oregon Territorial Legislature with the county seat at Port Townsend before Washington Territory was established. Sawmills were erected on the tidelands and company towns, built by early timber barons like Pope and Talbot, flourished. Manifest Destiny prevailed as many immigrants came west lured by the promise of making their fortunes. Settlers pushed on from the tide flats, penetrated the timbered valleys and open prairies on the peninsula. With axes and sweat, they put daylight in the swamp by hewing stump ranches out of the timbered bottomlands. Some stayed, but many left, victims of loneliness and the overpowering presence of the forest.

*Portage on the Quinault River with Indian Canoes, A.V. Higley and Clark Peeler, 1894*

*Hoquiam to Lake Quinault Mail Stages, Charlie Kelly (left), A.V. Higley (right) 1909*

*A.V. Higley with his violin, former Civil War drummer boy who pioneered Lake Quinault. Courtesy Orlo Higley Collection*

Port Townsend became the hub of commercial activity for all of Puget Sound because of its strategic location. Area settlers were threatened by the danger of Indian uprisings, but treaties were made with peninsula tribes at councils held at Medicine Creek, Point No Point and Neah Bay. Settlers continued to arrive, and soon a ring of pioneer settlements encircled the peninsula. Judge James G. Swan, former Indian teacher at Neah Bay, was appointed local agent at Port Townsend for the Northern Pacific Railroad Company; Puget Sound communities competed for the railroad terminus. Tacoma was chosen, and the Olympic Peninsula remained isolated. The mountain range in the interior—snow-covered, mysterious, and foreboding—proved to be a challenge for rugged explorers destined to be the last of the mountain men. Prospectors soon followed in search of gold and other minerals.

In 1885, young Lt. Joseph O'Neil was ordered to make a reconnaissance of the northeast section of the Olympic Mountains. His efforts were cut short by military orders to report to Ft. Leavenworth, Kansas. He returned five years later and completed a crossing of the Olympic Mountains from Lake Cushman to Lake Quinault with members of his party, exploring the Queets, Dosewallips, Duckabush, and Humptulips River drainages. The first successful overland journey through the untamed Olympics was the Press Expedition led by veteran explorer James H. Christie in 1889-1890. O'Neil, Christie, and other explorers attempted to resolve the ancient Indian legend about a mysterious godlike thunderbird which lived in the heart of the peninsula and repelled those who would enter its domain. The thunderbird continues to be a dominant force in Northwest Coast Indian Art traditions.

In 1891, one year after the interior of the Olympics had been explored, the president of the United States was given power to establish Forest Reserves from the public

*Mr. Herrick (Elwha Homesteader) Cougar Hunting. Photo by Herb Crisler, courtesy Ruby El Hult*

*Grant Humes, Homesteader/Packer at His Ranch on the Elwha, ca. 1922. Courtesy Klahhane Club*

*Bridge Across West Fork of Dosewallips River, ca. 1910*

*Early Days in Quilcene*

*Mr. & Mrs. Orte Higley (in 1907 Franklin), 1912*

domain. In 1897, the Olympic Forest Reserve was created by executive order, and Gifford Pinchot was sworn in as a Confidential Forest Agent to examine and report on the Forest Reserves. He visited Lake Crescent, hiked via Sol Duc Hot Springs to the Hoh River Divide, then down the Bogachiel with Al Blackwood, "A first-class woodsman."

> *It was a great trip. I believed then, and I may have been right, that white men had never passed that way before. At any rate, for three days, we saw no trace of humans, but only wolf tracks and the deep-worn trails of the Olympic Elk.*

As a result of Forester Pinchot's examination of the Western Reserves, he was able to set up a practical plan, nationwide, for the establishment of a Forest Service under the Department of Agriculture, with trained foresters administering forest lands. Theodore F. Rixon was a railroad surveyor who along with his partner, Arthur Dodwell, surveyed, cruised, and mapped the Olympic Forest Reserve from 1898-1900. Their report on forest conditions was published in 1902. Mr. Rixon was a man of such great integrity and expertise that he was given the title of Forest Expert. His packer during the monumental survey, Jack McGlone, was the first person to climb Mt. Olympus, in 1899. High points of Rixon's distinguished career with the Forest Service included mapping and cruising Forest Reserves in Arizona, New Mexico, Oregon, and Wyoming. He also surveyed summer home lots on Lake Crescent and Lake Quinault in 1910 and 1911. Mr. Rixon's Olympic accomplishments are honored by the naming of Dodwell-Rixon Pass in the mountains he and his partner surveyed. One time when coming down the Sol Duc trail, Mr. Rixon encountered a young woman pioneer living at Fairholme located at the West End of Lake Crescent.

*James H. Christie "Mountain Man" (Leader of the Press Expedition 1889-1890). Photo taken in Canada, ca. 1886, courtesy Ruby El Hult, The Untamed Olympics*

*Quinault Valley Pioneers. Left to right: front row, Roy Streator, Otto Kestner, Ransom Higley, A.V. Higley; back row, Ovid Milbourn, John Streator, Belle Donaldson, Maggie Higley, Thelma Carlson, Constance Olson*

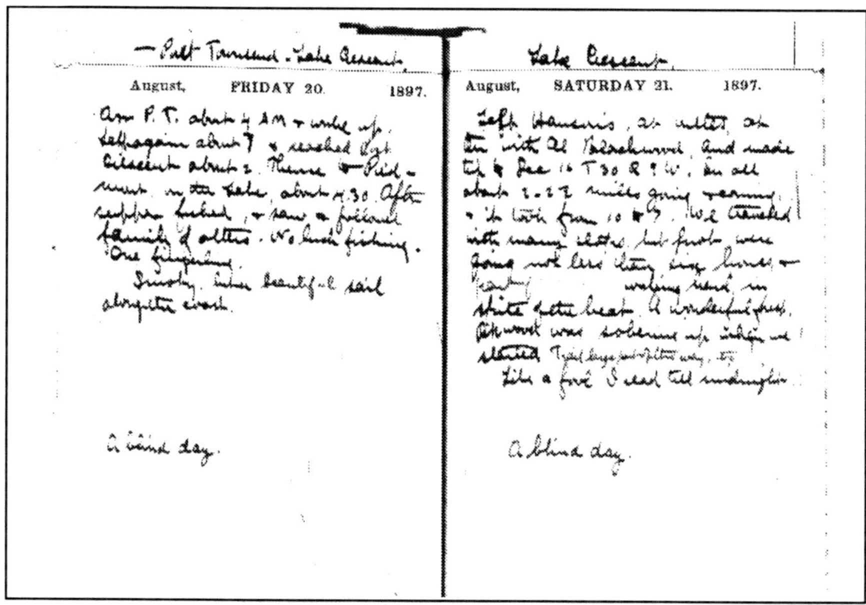
Port Townsend - Lake Crescent

August, FRIDAY 20. 1897.

A blind day.

Lake Crescent.

August, SATURDAY 21. 1897.

A blind day.

*Two Pages From Gifford Pinchot's Diary Noting Rainy, Perhaps Foggy Days, on the Olympic Peninsula*

They fell in love and he romantically named a mountain "Carrie" after her.

When the Forest Reserve was created, many settlers on the west end of the peninsula gave up their claims. Some lands were eliminated from the reserve and restored by proclamation to the public domain, resulting in the splendid forests of western Clallam County being acquired by timber companies and speculators.

*Early Railroad Logging in the Olympic National Reserves, 1897*
*Photo by Gifford Pinchot*

*A Rare, Vintage Photo of Forest Expert Theodore Rixon, Enjoying a Moment of Leisure at Lake Crescent*

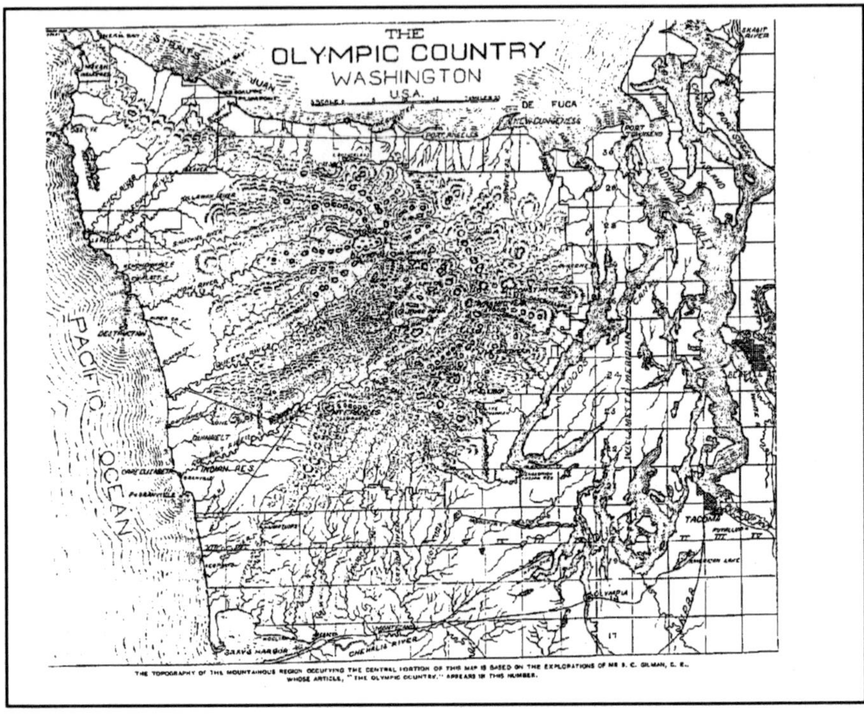


*Reprinted from the National Geographic Magazine, Vol. VII, No. 4, April, 1896*

*Theodore F. Rixon, Surveyor, and Chet Howser, Assistant District Ranger, Port Angeles Office, 1920s*

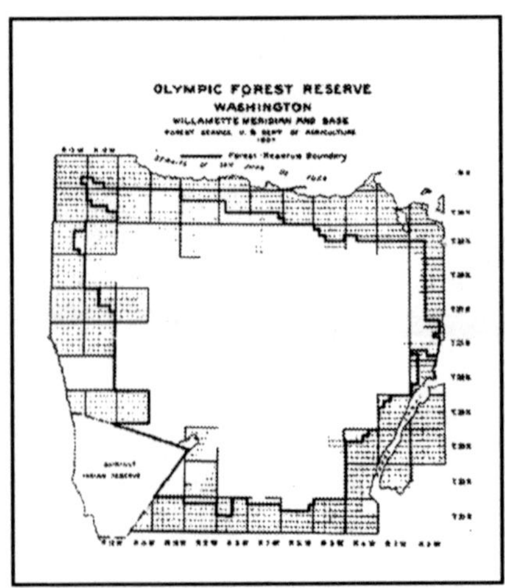

3306 PROCLAMATIONS, 1907.

March 2, 1907.

BY THE PRESIDENT OF THE UNITED STATES OF AMERICA

A PROCLAMATION

*Olympic Forest Reserve, Wash. Preamble. Vol. 29, p. 901. Vol. 31, p. 1962. Vol. 32, p. 1981.*

WHEREAS, the Olympic Forest Reserve, in the State of Washington, was established by proclamation dated February twenty-second, eighteen hundred and ninety-seven, and the boundaries thereof have been subsequently changed to exclude therefrom certain lands and also to include additional lands in the State of Washington;

And whereas it appears that the public good would be promoted by further adding to the said forest reserve certain lands, in the State of Washington, which are in part covered with timber;

*Boundaries further enlarged. Vol. 30, p. 30.*

Now, therefore, I, Theodore Roosevelt, President of the United States of America, by virtue of the power in me vested by the Act of Congress, approved June fourth, eighteen hundred and ninety-seven, entitled, "An Act Making appropriations for sundry civil expenses of the Government for the fiscal year ending June thirtieth, eighteen hundred and ninety-eight, and for other purposes," do proclaim that the aforesaid Olympic Forest Reserve is hereby enlarged to include the said additional lands, and that the boundaries of the reserve are now as shown on the diagram forming a part hereof;

*Lands excepted.*

Excepting from the force and effect of this proclamation all lands which are at this date embraced in any legal entry or covered by any lawful filing or selection duly of record in the proper United States Land Office, or upon which any valid settlement has been made pursuant to law, and the statutory period within which to make entry or filing of record has not expired; and also excepting all lands which at this date are embraced within any withdrawal or reservation for any use or purpose to which this reservation for forest uses is inconsistent: Provided, that these exceptions shall not continue to apply to any particular tract of land unless the entryman, settler, or claimant continues to comply with the law under which the entry, filing, or settlement was made, or unless the reservation or withdrawal

*Coal lands.*

to which this reservation is inconsistent continues in force; not excepting from the force and effect of this proclamation, however, any land within the boundary herein described, which has been withdrawn to protect the coal therein but this proclamation does not vacate any such coal land withdrawal; and provided that these exceptions shall not apply to any land embraced in any selection, entry or filing, which has been allowed or permitted to remain of record subject to the creation of a permanent reservation.

*Reserved from settlement.*

Warning is hereby given to all persons not to make settlement upon the lands reserved by this proclamation.

IN WITNESS WHEREOF, I have hereunto set my hand and caused the seal of the United States to be affixed.

Done at the City of Washington this 2d day of March, in the year of our Lord one thousand nine hundred and seven, and of [SEAL.] the Independence of the United States the one hundred and thirty-first.

THEODORE ROOSEVELT

By the President:
ELIHU ROOT
*Secretary of State.*

*Arthur Dodwell, of the Rixon-Dodwell Survey Team, First Surveyors of Olympic Reserve, 1898-1900. Courtesy J. Scharf*

*Theodore Rixon, Forest Expert. Courtesy Bob Rixon*

*Conservation of natural resources... is the key to the safety and prosperity of the American people, and of all the people of the world, for all time to come.*
*Gifford Pinchot*

Under the dynamic leadership of Gifford Pinchot, Chief Forester, the Conservation Movement was expanded and applied to natural resources. Emphasis was placed on administrative reorganization to prevent reckless land and resource exploitation. Pinchot placed local rangers in charge and monitoring was conducted by trained, competent inspectors.

The first real supervisor of the Olympic National Forest was Fred Hanson (1903-1909) who established his headquarters at Hoodsport. Chris Morgenroth was appointed Ranger in charge of the north portion of the Peninsula comprising most of Jefferson and all of Clallam County. Paul Laufield was the Ranger of the southern part of the Peninsula. In 1906, Hanson reported on information requested by Overton Price, Associate Forester under Chief Pinchot. A representative facsimile of his letter and enclosures follow:

*Hoodsport Washington.*
*August 1, 1906*
*Hon. The Forester*
*Forest Service*
*Washington, D.C.*

*Dear Sir:*
*In reply to your letter June 8, I respectfully enclose herewith report upon the standing of all the special privileges cases referred to in your letter of the above date.*

*Very truly yours,*
*Forest Supervisor*

—

1. *John A. Ewell, Quiniault, Washington. [sic]*
2. *February 4, 1902.*
3. *To occupy three acres of land in Lot 2, Section 20, Township 23 north, Range 9 West, W.M., and conduct a store and hotel in buildings already constructed thereon.*
4. *November 17, 1902.*
5. *Terminable at the discretion of the Forester.*
6. *$1,000.*

*The above privilege have been surrendered by J.A. Ewell, and the property is now included in the lease of R.L. and, A.V. Higley, for Lot 2, Sec. 20, Tp. 23, N.R. 9 west, W.M., and the privilege is still continued for store, hotel and Post-Office, Permit 12-23-05., rental per annum $10.00, Bond $250.*

*The above property is included in the list of sites for Rangers quarters, but that the property may be leased until such time it is needed by the Service. [sic]*

*Clarence Adams, Forest Clerk*

—

1. *Earnest E. Fishel, Quiniault Washington. [sic]*
2. *April 25, 1903.*
3. *To occupy a stable and fence three acres of land in Lot 2, Section 30, Township 23 north, Range 9 west, W.M., to facilitate the carrying of mail.*
4. *June 15, 1903.*
5. *Terminable at the discretion of the Forester.*
6. *No bond.*

*The above privilege is not used and the property is included in the list of sites for Rangers quarters, and should be canceled, the applicant Earnest E. Fishel is now serving as Assistant Forest Ranger at Quiniault, Wash. [sic]*

—

1. *Henry Littleton, Piedmont, Wash.*
2. *June 11, 1904.*
3. *To operate a steamboat on Lake Crescent, in Township 30 north, Ranges 8 and 9 West, W.M.*
4. *October 7, 1904.*
5. *Terminable at the discretion of the Forester.*
6. *No bond.*

*The above privilege have been in operation continuously ever since permit was granted carrying freight and passengers to different points on the lake, this business is small, and not very profitable, and is more for accommodation, and I recommend that this permit be continued without bond or rental for the following reasons, Mr. Littleton have never made any charges for carrying any Government tools or freight on the lake, and never makes any charges for Forest Officers when traveling on his boat, and that he is always ready to assist or give information to Forest Officers of anything that will be of interest to the Service. [sic]*

*The Supervisor's Staff Performing Administrative Tasks in February 1909*

In 1906, Forest Inspector W. T. Cox, accompanied by Supervisor Fred Hanson, walked a total of 360 miles in the Forest Reserve, camping out where necessary. Averaging 20 miles a day, they carried "Queets Indian pack saddles" made of spruce strips and cross pieces to which they cinched their regular packs. Inspector Cox remarked:

*It was grievous to see literally billions of feet of timber that had been eliminated from the Olympic National Forest…we saw scarcely a cabin on our trip through the lands in question. That elimination from the Olympic was perhaps the biggest robbery of a National Forest ever pulled off.*

He also commented on the elk of the Olympics. That same year, 1906, marked the first timber sales on the east and west forks of the Humptulips River. The Humptulips Driving Company was issued a special use permit for setting up a dam site. The logs were transported by a splash dam downriver to Grays Harbor and the hungry mills on the tide flats.

*The Quinault Lodge as it Appeared After Addition of the East Wing, Sometime Prior to 1923. Courtesy Higley Family*

Supervisor Hanson was demoted to ranger at Hoodsport and replaced by R. E. Benedict whose major contribution was to hire Clarence Adams as forest clerk. Mr. Adams served the Olympic well. In 1912, during the administration of Mr. Parish Lovejoy, Clarence Adams was appointed draftsman and completed the first

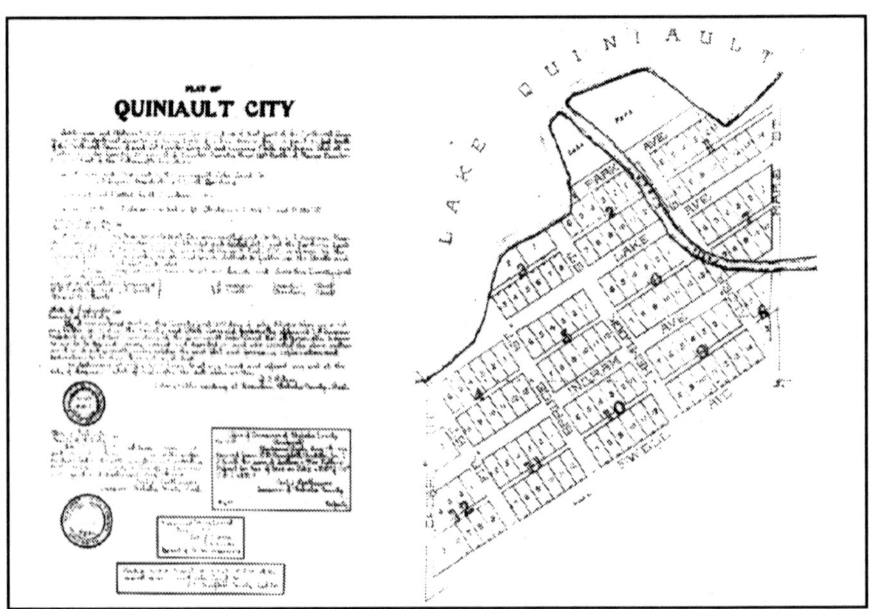


*Plat of Quinault, 1903*

map of the Olympic National Forest. He became Administrative Assistant on the Olympic and was the original keeper of historical records for most forest activities.

The field crew on the Olympic during the years 1904-1908 consisted of the following personnel, most of whom were hired as seasonal forest guards:

E. G. Newman .................................... 1904
Fred J. Ferris ...................................... 1904
E. J. Finch ......................................... 1904
B. J. Northup ..................................... 1904
J. Denny Ahl ......................................1905
John Dyke............................................1905
C. P. Nutter ........................................1905
E. E. Fishel ......................................... 1906
James L. Bixby ................................... 1906
Edward M. Cheney ...............................1907
Albian J. Finch ................................... 1908
W. T. Strait ......................................... 1908
Ernest R. Paull ................................... 1908

These early forest guards encountered various local problems among the settlers, some of whom worked for the Forest Service building and maintaining trails. Wagon roads were developed in the settlements as people became less dependent on water routes for transportation. Fire regulations and procedures were adopted as well as authorizations and guidelines for timber uses. In 1907, the Interrorem Guard Station was constructed by Emory J. Finch of Hoodsport. The oldest structure on the Olympic National Forest, it is still utilized seasonally and is an outstanding log structure representative of the pioneer tradition. Twenty-four ranger stations or guard stations were listed on the historic 1912 map drafted by Clarence Adams. None of the original buildings exist today except Interrorem on the Duckabush River. Chris Morgenroth was instrumental in the construction of a two-story log cabin on Lake Crescent in 1909. This cabin, named after Chris, was also known as Storm King Ranger Station for many years. It was abandoned by officials from the Olympic National Park and replaced with a replica at a nearby location. In 1908, Gifford Pinchot selected Port Townsend to be the location of Olympic National Forest headquarters. However, this was not implemented. Olympia was chosen as the preferred alternative in 1909, because of its central location with a railroad terminus. This coincided with the establishment of the Mt. Olympus National Monument when President Theodore Roosevelt proclaimed the center of the Forest a 615,000-acre refuge for the Olympic elk.

The heavily-timbered lands in Clallam County were the target for exploitation, with four railroad companies competing for the best right-of-way location. Theodore Rixon was employed as chief surveyor for the Northern Pacific, and with a crew of fifty men, explored routes from Grays Harbor, via Ozette Lake, to Port Angeles.

*Intermount Ranger Station, South Fork Skokomish River, ca. 1912*

*Duckabush Guard Station, ca. 1908*

*Louella Guard Station, Quilcene Ranger District, Built by E. M. Cheney (Named for His Wife) ca. 1912*

*Graves Creek Station, Ranger Joe Fulton (left), 1927*

*Interrorem Ranger Station, Ed Newman (right), Mr. Pierce (center), Mrs. Pierce (2nd from left), Resort Owners on the Duckabush, 1907*

*Olympus Ranger Station, Ranger Sanford Floe Issues Campfire Permit, September 1927*

*Deer Lake Guard Station, Howard Johnson, 1927*

*Eagle Guard Station (Constructed in 1923) Sol Duc Hot Springs Road, Prickett (left), Bill Davis (right) September 1927*

*Guard/Patrolman Charlie Lewis Splitting Spruce, September 1927*

*Lincoln Guard Station Staircase Camp, North Fork Skokomish, September 1926*

*Lincoln Guard Station, Landscaping, November 6, 1935*

*Deer Park Guard Station, ca. 1922*

*Campbell's Mine Shelter, West Fork Humptulips River, June 1930*

*Camp Marion (Built by Fay Bunnell) on the Dosewallips Trail, Used by Hikers and Campers in the Olympics*

*Snow Creek Guard Station, 1929*

*Storm King Ranger Station, ca. 1909, Chris Morgenroth (2nd from left), Paul Laufeld (extreme right)*

*Slab Camp Guard Station, 1931*

*Quilcene Ranger Station, 1931*

*On the Elwha–Chet Howser, Forest Service Trail Crew Member (left), John Tolan, Trail Foreman, ca. 1923. Herb Crisler Collection, courtesy Ruby El Hult*

LEGEND FOR MAP SHOWING THE PROPOSED NEW DISTRICTS.

Each administrative unit, regardless of actual National Forest boundaries, shown in same shade. For example see Sawtooth National Forest and Payette National Forest, Idaho; or Grand Canyon National Forest, South, San Francisco Mountains National Forest, and Black Mesa National Forest, Arizona.

Explorers
Trappers
Indian Chiefs

We ought to commemorate the men who made the West.

I have checked the names to which I object. Please try to find others of one word each. I would [illegible] names of natural features or of explorers, trappers, Indians, & one forest should be named Roosevelt & one Wilson. GP

| | | | |
|---|---|---|---|
| 93 | — | Sierra (North) | Northfork |
| 94 | — | Sierra (South) | Hot Springs |
| 95 | | Inyo | Bishop |
| 96 | | Monterey<br>Pinnacles | Salinas |
| 97 | — | San Luis Obispo | San Luis Obispo |
| 98 | | Santa Barbara | Santa Barbara |
| 99 | | San Gabriel<br>San Bernardino | Los Angeles |
| 100 | —| San Jacinto<br>Trabuco Canyon | Hemet |

Oregon

? As at present. *Fremont should be retained somewhere*

Washington

| | | | |
|---|---|---|---|
| 101 | | Columbia | Vancouver *St. Helens* |
| 102 | | Rainier | Orting |
| 103 | | Snoqualmie | Snohomish |
| 104 | — | Mt. Baker *Skagit* | Sedro Woolley *Skagit?* |
| 105 | | Methow | Twisp |
| 106 | | Chelan | Wenatchee |
| 107 | | Yakima (with Rainier) | Orting |
| 108 | | Olympic | Port Townsend |
| 109 | | Colville | Republic |
| 110 | | Wenaha | Walla Walla |

Alaska

? As at present.

-7-

*Excerpts From Page 1 and Page 7 in Official "Redistricting Records" Showing Personal Comments by Gifford Pinchot*

*Wynoochee Guard Station, Forest Officers E.J. (Ed) Hanzlik (right), J.O.F. Anderson (left), August 8, 1938*

*...At first, the frontier was the Atlantic coast. It was the frontier of Europe and in a very real sense moving westward, the frontier became more and more American... [sic]*

*Frederick Jackson Turner*

The outstanding figure in the earliest days of the Olympic National Forest was the remarkable Chris Morgenroth, a German emigrant, who worked his passage while aboard a ship heading to New York. He arrived, penniless, at the age of fifteen, but was befriended by a bachelor from the "old country" who drove a horse-drawn cab. Chris groomed the horse and assisted the passengers in exchange for board and room.

He headed west and while job hunting on the Seattle waterfront, was shanghaied by seal-fur hunters heading for Alaska. Almost two years passed during which the vessel sold the contraband pelts in various ports in the Orient. When the crew was captured, they were taken back to Seattle for trial. Chris was eventually exonerated and left the sea for the woods, working as a lumberjack at Port Orchard. He later chose to homestead on the Bogachiel. When the Forest Reserve was created, Chris supplemented his income with temporary, seasonal work with the Forest Service. Chris, according to a firsthand account was "built like a bull elk, quite stocky with powerful legs." Those legs were destined to travel many miles in the Olympics.

Mr. Morgenroth's first assigned duty upon entering the Forest Service June 15, 1903, was locating and building a trail along the south side of Lake Crescent and along the Soleduck River to the settlement of Sappho. There it connected with the road from Clallam Bay to Forks. This trail location was later used as the route for the present highway which connects Port Angeles with the west end of Clallam and Jefferson counties and which forms an important link for the Olympic Loop.

Morgenroth was truly a man of action and his notorious adventures and experiences in the Olympic wilderness rivaled the earlier exploits of the Christie and the O'Neil expeditions. The district ranger's office was in the Morse Building in Port Angeles while the present Snider Work Center was established as a field station in 1915. The Snider Ranger Station site was the former Homestead Entry #19028 of January 28, 1905, filed by Mr. Finly Apple.

*Olympic Forest Supervisor Parish Lovejoy, Hoh River, 1911*

*Capt. George Whitehead, First Quilcene Ranger, ca. 1912*

Morgenroth had married a "schoolmarm" in Port Angeles where they became active in local society. Chris was among the dozen guests aboard the first passenger train trip from Port Angeles to Sequim in 1915. He and his wife became members of the Klahane Club, the Olympic mountaineering group formed that same year. The distinguished surveyor and forest expert, Theodore Rixon and his fair lady from Fairholme, were also members. The major force in the Klahane Club was the prominent outdoorsman, sportsman and newspaper publisher, E. B. Webster. The Klahane Club was originally located at the site of the Louis Williams cabin, which at the time was within the boundaries of the expansive Olympic Forest Reserve. A special use permit was issued to the Klahane Club by Supervisor Fromme and a long and fruitful association began (Klahane means "good times out-of-doors" in the Chinook jargon).

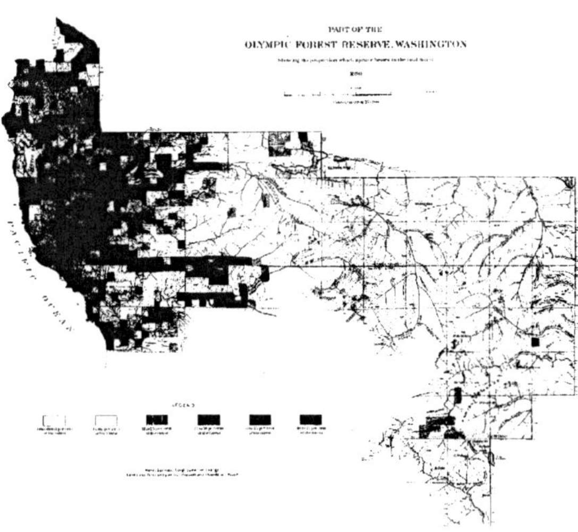

*Map From the 1902 Dodwell Rixon Report "Forest Conditions in the Olympic Reserve"*

By 1910, according to Parish Lovejoy, the supervisor of the Olympic National Forest, many improvements had been completed including the construction of the Louella Ranger Station near Quilcene and the

*Morgenroth (3rd from left) at Snider Ranger Station in 1922 with Oliver Erickson, Assistant Forest Supervisor (far left), and Fred Ames, Assistant Regional Forester (2nd from left)*

*E. E. Fishel, First Ranger at Quinault, and (Later) Assistant Forest Supervisor, ca. 1945*

Norwood Ranger Station above Lake Quinault. Earnest E. Fishel had been the first ranger at Norwood/ Quinault but promptly quit in 1910 to homestead the "Quinault Burn," later known as Neilton. He was succeeded by E. R. Paull who helped build a pioneer trail from Quinault to Killea Ranger Station on the Queets River and the Humptulips-Wynoochee Trail. J. O. Anderson was responsible for patrolling the area from the Clearwater River to Lake Crescent 1909-1911. He traveled by foot and by horseback as trails were few. Ralph Hiligoss was ranger at Hoodsport from 1910 until 1943 when he left the Forest Service and took over administration of the Simpson Logging Company timber sales. Captain George Whitehead was the first ranger at Quilcene 1910-1918. Originally, the headquarters were in the building on Main Street that now houses the liquor store. According to Robert L. Wood, author of the historical *Accounts of the O'Neil and Press Expeditions*:

> *From 1910 to 1918, Whitehead explored every stream between Port Angeles and Hoodsport and named many streams after Army officers who went with him. Burdick Creek was named for a Lieutenant Burdick, Knerr Creek was named for General Kneer [sic] and Hayden Pass was named for Colonel John L. Hayden, commanding officer of the Army post (Fort Worden) at Port Townsend. Whitehead insisted that officers sit down in the creek before he would name it after them.*

*Forest Service Trail Crew, Quinault, 1910. Left to right: unidentified, Chester Wilson, Ranger E. R. Paull, Bonney, Watson, unidentified (in wagon)*

During the last century there was a military trail built from Discovery Bay to the vicinity of Slab Camp. This trail was built for the purpose of subjugating the Indians. The trail was about 12 feet wide. Capt. Whitehead, when asked, said the trail was all but obscured during his period on the Olympic. He said the trail

*Ranger Hilligoss*

started at Ed Brown's farm near Maynard, but he did not know where it went from there. The map enclosure of "Forest Conditions in the Olympic Forest Reserve" by Arthur Dodwell and Theodore Rixon, 1902, shows a military trail in the north portion of T. 28 N., R. 3 W., in a drainage which appears to be Gold Creek. The map does not show anything east of Range 3.

Supervisor Lovejoy was on the Olympic National Forest for only two years, but he was able to utilize his experience on the devastating forest fires in Montana in 1910 and to recognize the potential fire hazards on the Olympic. He also appreciated the value of Theodore Rixon and Ranger Morgenroth of whom he said: "...my ideas have largely been absorbed from Morgenroth who is the best fire fighter in the country if not the world." In a 1912 memo to his successor Fromme, Lovejoy had written a detailed account outlining his concerns. His general plan for fire protection included:

> *Trails and trails and trails all looping into one another and into one another and into roads so as to allow cross cuts. All main trails and roads, and bye and bye all trails and roads paralleled with phone lines. Patrol boxes not farther than 5 miles apart on the phone lines. Boxes and lots of tools at or near the patrol tel stations. Houses and sheds and shelters along the trails where they will serve to shelter crews and patrolmen and all traveling officers and where the tools in the boxes can be concentrated winters and protected. Think this very important. We have made a fair start to the shelters this season and the boys have the idea and will develop if it encourages. Then lots of guards and as nearly as possible regular beats and times, morning tests of the phone lines, specific arrangements for repair in case of trouble. Then lookouts. Benedict ridiculed the idea when I suggested it. I think the rangers are about converted to it now and*

*Chris Morgenroth, 1908. Courtesy Katherine Flaherty*

*On a Long Hike—Parish Lovejoy and Charlie Anderson, 1911. Courtesy Katherine Flaherty*

*several seem certain and have their points selected. These should be looked over carefully and mapped so as to get right location and so as to show the country commanded from each, slopes etc. This work should be done carefully so as to get good base lines and allow the working out of the triangulation of the base map. Walker Mt (Dist 2) and Baldy in Dist 4 should be equipped for next year if they check up as well as they have been reported. [sic]*

*The Road to Forks Before the Big Fire of 1907. Courtesy Bert Kellogg*

Parish Lovejoy went on to greater achievement returning to his alma mater, Michigan, as Assistant Professor of Forestry where he was recognized as an outstanding teacher. His work for the Michigan Department of Conservation invited more lucrative and prestigious offers of employment elsewhere. However, he declined, to stay in Michigan as chief advisor on land use problems. Lovejoy met another Forest Service supervisor of outstanding merit in 1925. His name has become synonymous with conservation, wilderness and land management: Aldo Leopold. They became friends and carried on a lively correspondence for seventeen years. Parish Lovejoy is credited with being the most direct, significant influence on Aldo Leopold in his original creative approach to ecological principles. In the 1942 *Journal of Wildlife Management* an obituary written by Leopold appeared with these words: "I believe that P. S. Lovejoy sired more ideas about men and land than any contemporary in the conservation field."

*The Puncheon Road to Lake Quinault, 1913. Photo by Fromme*

The successor to Parish Lovejoy was the remarkable Rudo Fromme. During a thirty-eight-year career in the Forest

Service, his longest assignment was on the Olympic, from 1912-1926. While attending Purdue University in 1902, he was attracted to forestry after reading an article by Gifford Pinchot.

During the summers Rudo sandwiched in work at lumber camps in West Virginia and North Carolina, earning $.85 per day. He attended the 1904 session of the Yale Forest School at Milford, Pennsylvania, and received his Masters Degree in Forestry from Yale in 1906. At one of the weekly Wednesday baseball games that summer, Fromme recalled that he pitched for the fledgling foresters and the opposing pitcher was the Chief of the Forest Service, Gifford Pinchot. Rudo passed the Civil Service examination immediately following graduation and became a Junior Forester assigned to the Priest River Forest Reserve in Idaho and Washington State. Subsequent assignments in San Francisco (as Chief of Operations and Personnel Officer) and two forests in Oregon, preceded his transfer to Olympia. He accomplished a personal goal when he was selected as supervisor of the Olympic because he valued its reputation for having the most timber and the least fire danger.

Rudo Fromme was an extremely versatile man, skilled in photography, drafting, writing, and public speaking in addition to his forester background. His experiences on the Olympics have been faithfully recorded in his Forest Service memoirs. His initiation to this vast mountainous land under his jurisdiction was an eye—opener:

> *Automobile travel was impossible for reaching Hood Canal, or the eastern side of the Forest, when I first reached Olympia. It was also of no practical value to the west side either and there was a daily bus, or small mail stage, to Humptulips. From there to Quinault Lake was the old Puncheon Road, which only a horse-drawn light buggy or buckboard would attempt to bounce over.*
>
> *Therefore, to reach any part of Hood Canal or the Straits side of the Olympic Peninsula, the most feasible route was to Seattle and from there by steamship. There were a few short stretches of narrow, rough wagon road along the Forest to get a launch. Within a year or so of my arrival, we purchased a used cabin cruiser from a Seattle sportsman and used it, not only for passenger and freight duty, but also as a traveling lookout in fire danger weather.*
>
> *There were two steamers out of Seattle for Port Townsend and Port Angeles, the well equipped Sol Duc, with state rooms, which left at midnight, and the Wielealie (pronounced Wy-ee-lee-ay-lie) but usually referred to as the Weary Willie. It was more strictly a freight boat and very unreliable as to time schedules. Coming back to Seattle, the Sol Duc left at 7:00 or 8:00 am., thus making round trip each 24 hours, Sundays included. There was a short railroad operating daily both ways from Port Townsend to Port Angeles, with frequent stops between.*
>
> *To the west from Port Angeles, one could take the Stanley Steamer Stage, an 8 or 10 seated automobile, if I remember the size correctly. It ferried across Lake Crescent, with Sol Duc*

> *Hot Spring Hotel as its destination, more popular around 1912, and several years later, with Canadians than with Americans. The town of Forks, or the Quileute Indian Village at La Push (on the ocean) could be reached only by a very poor wagon trail, safer by horseback, or on foot. [sic]*

Fromme was a very civic-minded person, active in the Elks Club, Kiwanis, Chamber of Commerce, and in charge of local dances, sponsored by the State Legislature, and the Governor's Inaugural Ball. But he was definitely a field man who was able to establish a rapport with the settler, the logger, the townspeople who lived on the Olympic Peninsula. He was remembered by Orlo Higley, of the pioneer family at Quinault, as being:

*Stanley Steamers on Road to Sol Duc Hot Springs 1914*

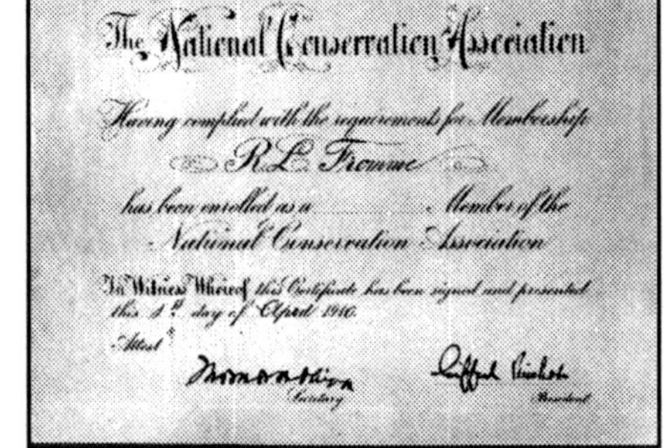

The National Conservation Association

Having complied with the requirements for Membership

R.L. Fromme

has been enrolled as a Member of the National Conservation Association

In Witness Whereof this Certificate has been signed and presented this 1st day of April 1910.

Attest

Secretary

Gifford Pinchot

President

*Rudo Fromme (1st on left, front row) and His 1906 Yale Classmates, Which Included Future Forest Service Leaders, Fred Ames, Assistant Regional Forester PNW (next to Rudo), and Chiefs Robert Stuart and Henry S. Graves (second row, 4th from left, and fourth row, 1st on left respectively)*

*A very lively fellow, congenial, kinda comical.*

Fromme was able to deal effectively with the forest fire situation by establishing a fire prevention program, using lectures and lantern slides and skits involving parodies of popular songs. One of the major areas of concern for the new supervisor was the agitation on the part of the Mountaineer's Club in Seattle and the Chambers of Commerce in Grays Harbor towns to transfer the scenic interior of the Olympic National Forest to National Park Status:

*"Friend of the Forest," E. B. Webster, Port Angeles Newspaper Editor, Sportsman, Author*

*So far as I could learn, no Forest officer had openly confronted this agitation excepting District Ranger Chris Morgenroth to a mild extent to the Klah-hane Club (mountain-climbing) of Port Angeles, his district.*

*I considered this a problem of real precedence, aside from getting acquainted with the District Rangers, their major problems and the more accessible areas of each District, which wasn't much. I called on the main officers of the Seattle Mountaineers, got myself and wife an invitation to join their 1913 Olympic Outing, a trek by foot and pack horses, through the Forest, north to south—up*

*The SYLVA Floating Fire Lookout, Earl McCardle, Skipper, ca. 1915. Special Collections, University of Washington*

# *The Many Faces*

*Prepared for Airplane Flight, 1921*

*Aerial Surveillance, Fromme and Pilot, ca. 1921*

*Rudo Fromme—Mounted Patrol*

# of Rudo Fromme

*Rudo Fromme, Chris Morgenroth (in Doorway) Kloshe Nanitch Lookout, ca. 1921. Courtesy Katherine Flaherty*

*"The Dynamic Duo" Rudo Fromme (left) and Chris Morgenroth (right), ca. 1917*

*Supervisor Rudo Fromme, 1918*

*the Elwha River and down the N. Fork Quinault, with side trip climb of Mt. Olympus and other prominent peaks adjacent to the main route, and succeeded in getting their unqualified endorsement of National Forest administration of the entire area. This was repeated in 1920, although other Forest matters prevented my starting with them, and I had to catch up with them by horse back after they had gone one week. [sic]*

Fromme cultivated a good relationship with the public by his social appearances and was in great demand as a speaker. He was a natural entertainer and humorist and served the Forest Service well in the field of public relations, not just on the Olympic but on his other forest assignments. By cooperating with the mountaineering groups such as the Klahane Club and the Seattle Mountaineers, he was able to further the aims of the forest ethic: service for the greatest number; utilization of all resources, and scientific management of the forest. E. B. Webster, publisher of the Port Angeles Evening News and president of the Klahane Club, broached Rudo Fromme about the establishment of a Mt. Angeles game sanctuary within the national forest and adjacent area. Portions of the letter in response convey the spirit and intent of the Forest Service (as follows):

*On the Skokomish, 1920*

*In the Field With Olympic Fire Guards, ca. 1918.*
*Photos pages 20-21 Special Collections, University of Washington*

*Rudo Fromme With His Olympic Packsack, Head of the Dosewallips, 1918. Special Collections, University of Washington*

*Rudo Fromme (center) Town Meeting, ca. 1917*

*Fish & Game, Olympic*
*Cooperation*

*May 25, 1920*

*Clallam County Game Commission,*
*Port Angeles, Washington*

*Gentlemen:*

*Several weeks ago, Mr. E. B. Webster, as President of the Klahane Club, called my attention to the advisability of creating a game preserve to embrace the main peaks of Mt. Angeles and most of the north slope. The reason which he advanced in support of this action appealed to me commendable and I suggested that he confer with ranger Morgenroth and the two of them take the proposition up with your commission. This course appears to have been followed according to a note from Morgenroth dated April 5, in which he states that you agreed to include as an addition to the National Forest area to be set aside also a strips one mile wide adjacent to the Forest boundary to include sections 32 to 36, inclusive, T. 30 N., R. 6 W., W.M.*

*All of the above information has been placed before the District Forester at Portland, together with our recommendations, and I am now authorized to request on behalf of the Forest Service and in the interest of game protection and propagation that the following described National Forest land be set aside as a State Game Preserve, wherein no game birds or game animals can be caught or killed with the boundaries thereof for such time and so longs as you may see fit and proper...* [sic]

*The exterior boundary of the area just described is surveyed with the exception of about 3 miles on the west side, but his line can no doubt be established sufficient for proper posting by your taking the matter up with Ranger Morgenroth, to whom a copy of this letter is being mailed.* [sic]

*...The special use business on any National Forest arises from the fact that all lands have for some natural or artificial reason greater value along some one line than any other, and in order to encourage this–the highest use–special permits are issued. On the Olympic, there are now nearly 100 such permits in effect, most of which are for lots for summer residence purposes on the shores of Lake Crescent and Queniult... [sic]*

*Supervisor R. L. Fromme*

Fromme's justification for special use permits was in keeping with Forest Service policy under Chief Forester Gifford Pinchot and his successor, formerly Dean of the Yale Forestry School, Henry Graves. Pinchot's dismissal as Chief Forester was politically motivated but with the selection of Graves, the integrity of the Forest Service was not compromised in any way. Henry Graves met with his former graduate student, Rudo Fromme, on a special trip to the Olympic National Forest in 1914. The purpose of this personal reconnaissance by the Chief Forester was to determine if too much timber and mineral opportunities were tied up in the Mt. Olympus National Monument.

*In Mt. Olympus National Monument, 1914. Left to right: George Cecil, District Forester; Frank Stannard, Mining Engineer; Henry Graves, Chief of U.S. Forest Service*

In May, 1915, President Wilson eliminated from the Mt. Olympus Monument 334,000 acres by proclamation. This was a direct result of Chief Forester Graves' trip. Supervisor Fromme, District Forester George Cecil, and mining promoter, F. H. Stannard of Seattle, had accompanied the chief forester, departing on horseback from Hood Canal. Ranger Hilligoss escorted them to the Success Creek Divide and a rendezvous with Ranger E. R. Paull who had misread instructions mailed earlier, and the entire party spent a miserable wet night. Supervisor Fromme consequently "thought it appropriate to commemorate the ordeal by changing 'Success' (Creek) to Graves Creek." [sic]

*Sol Duc Hot Springs Resort, 1914*

During Rudo Fromme's fourteen–year span on the Olympic, certain historic events stand out:

*Webb Logging Company "Show" Left to right: Supervisor Fromme, George Webb, Fred Ames (Regional Forest Officer and Former Yale Classmate of Fromme), Donkey Engineer (Unidentified). Special Collections, University of Washington*

1913 Mike Earles, the peninsula timber baron, had purchased the Sol Duc Hot Springs from the heirs of Theodore Moritz. The Forest Service had granted a road right-of-way and a magnificent hotel was erected. However, a timber trespass had been committed. Fromme personally collected for damages after the third visit to the lumberman's Seattle office.

1914 John Tornow, a desperado, wanted for killing two deputy sheriffs and two cousins, had holed up in the Wynoochee watershed. A sheriff's posse apprehended him in a forest–guard cabin hideaway.

1915 Mr. Fromme's graphic encounter with the notorious I.W.W. (Industrial Workers of the World) sums up the situation:

*These men were a menace to the war effort by urging strikes on one pretext or another. Three agitators entered the Webb sale of government timber on Jimmy-Come-Lately Creek one afternoon, without being aware that the loggers were partly engaged in burning slash as required by the F.S. contract. Mr Webb, the purchaser, telephoned me at dinner time, and I promised to call the sheriff in Port Angeles and urge that they be arrested and taken before the U.S. District Attorney in Seattle. I met the whole group there in the morning, Webb, the Sheriff and the three I.W.W.s. The latter were said to have been treating the matter as a lark, until I read some of the federal laws pertaining to interference with fire fighting and the timber sale operator's obligations. Then, they began to look more serious and asked me, as well as Mr Webb, some questions. [sic]*

*Well, this resulted in a much larger trial than anyone had anticipated. These arrested men succeeded in making it a trial of the entire I.W.W. movement. Before it was over, their local attorney had for assistance in person, the famous trial lawyer, Clarence Darrow to the defense, also subpoenas on District Forester Silcox and Chief of Operation Rutledge to vouch for the cooperative help they had gotten from the I.W.W. on recent fires out of the Missoula Montana office. By this time, I had gotten our Portland attorney, Mr Staley, and he, with the Seattle District attorney, managed to get the Trial Judge to forbid their testimony on the grounds that this was a trial of three individual men, who interfered with fire suppression of a government logging operation, where unburned slash was a dangerous menace, and being burned in a careful manner by experienced men under contract requirements of the Forest Service. The three men were sentenced to the McNeil Island Prison for a year and a day largely on the expert witness of the timber sale ranger, Everett Harpham. [sic]*

When the United States was drawn into World War I, airplanes were the newest weapon in the allied arsenal. The airplanes were mainly constructed of spruce which was strong, durable yet light in weight. The remote coastal forest of the Olympic contained most of the immediate supply of the versatile Sitka spruce needed for the war effort. The work situation in the lumber camps was unfavorable to meet the critical targets imposed by the military crisis in Europe. Unsanitary work conditions and the unstable work force of transient lumberjacks fueled the labor movement known as the Industrial Workers of the World (popularly called the "Wobblies") who organized strikes and reprisals such as the fire-fighting incident thwarted by Supervisor Fromme. The war in the woods was fought in a unique manner with the establishment of the Spruce Production Division under the direction of General Brice P. Disque. Composed of 30,000 men, the Spruce Army labored in tent camps where the highest concentrations of spruce were located: Lake Quinault, Lake Crescent, and the Hoko country were prime areas adjacent to, if not within the Olympic National Forest.

*Quinault Pioneers Knitting Sweaters for Soldiers During World War I. Left to right: Teander Olson, Fritz Halbert, Orlo Higley, Chester Wilson*

General Disque also organized a patriotic union known as the Loyal Legion of Loggers and Lumberman to combat the extreme unsanitary conditions and morale problems of the work force.

*Webb Logging Company. Special Collections, University of Washington*

A massive railroad and mill construction project was initiated by the Siems-Carey Company. The Spruce Railroad didn't haul one stick nor had the mill saws bitten into one spruce before the armistice was signed.

*Herb Crisler as an 18 Year Old Spruce Division Soldier/Aerial Photographer. He Filmed Disney's* Olympic Elk *and was an AWS Lookout During WWII. Courtesy Ruby El Hult*

While building the Spruce Division Railroad around Lake Crescent, Supervisor Fromme disagreed with General Disque about the location. Mr. Fromme contended that the preliminary railroad location along the shoreline interfered with the existing privately owned resorts or special use permits. The general argued that the emergency war situation justified the resorts and summer home losses. It was to end in a victory for General Disque and his spruce soldiers.

Another incident during World War I involved the FBI investigation of forest rangers Chris Morgenroth and George Whitehead, solely because of their German backgrounds. Affidavits were taken from army officers and prominent local people to vouch for their credibility. Ranger Whitehead resigned his position when the war escalated and he volunteered for sea duty in the merchant marine.

Rudo Fromme had been detailed to Alaska as replacement for the current supervisor who was scheduled for army induction. When the incumbent supervisor failed his army examination, Fromme returned to the Olympic. In 1921, he encountered the second most violent storm in Olympic history with hurricane force winds knocking down an estimated 8 billion board feet of timber. As a result of this big blowdown, additional fire protection funds were allocated to the Olympic. Additional trails were planned and built by well-experienced men like Henry Huelsdonk, brother of John, the famous "Iron man of the Hoh," his brother-in-law, Charlie Lewis, and Oscar Peterson who was the packer. Ralph McClanahan was the trail builder and fire fighter who helped Joe Fulton at Quilcene. In 1924, Fulton transferred to Quinault where Joe Kestner, Orlo

*Quinault District Ranger, Roy Muncaster (right) (Later Aboard a Vessel Torpedoed Off the Coast of Ireland)*

*Spruce Division Camp, Cook Creek, 1917/18*

*4th of July Celebration, WWI Spruce Division Soldiers, 1918*

*Splitting Spruce, Lake Quinault Area, 1917/1918*

*A Spruce Division Truck Traveling Across a Plank Road Near Forks ca. 1918. Courtesy Bert Kellogg*

*Spruce Division Constructing the Port Angeles Western Railroad in 1917. Courtesy Bert Kellogg*

*Spruce Squadron Camp, Near Lake Pleasant*

*Quilcene Ranger Joe Fulton and His Fort Lewis Fire Fighters (Army Soldiers Who Were Conscientious Objectors During World War I). Special Collections, University of Washington*

*Charlie Lewis "Off Duty." Courtesy Marilyn Lewis, Charlie's Daughter*

*Charlie Lewis "In the Big Timber." Courtesy Marilyn Lewis, Charlie's Daughter*

*Bill Whitcomb, Joe Lyendecker, Chris Lyendecker, Louise Whitcomb, Oscar Peterson*

*Pete Brandenberry, Bogachiel Guard Station*

*From left to right; Marie Huelsdonk, Unidentified, Marie's Uncle Henry Huelsdonk*

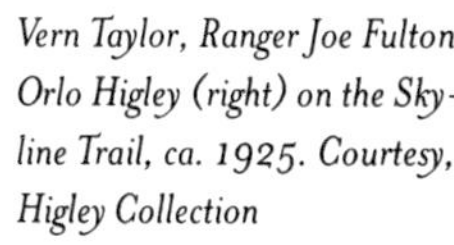

*Vern Taylor, Ranger Joe Fulton, Orlo Higley (right) on the Skyline Trail, ca. 1925. Courtesy, Higley Collection*

*Chris Morgenroth Inspecting 1921 Blowdown Along Trail*

*Aftermath of 1921 Blowdown*

*Ralph McClanahan, Forest Guard/Fire Fighter (Later CCC Foreman), Quilcene*

*Inspecting the Blowdown, Chris Morgenroth, 1921*

*Charlie Lewis Using Old #9-wire Telephone Line. Photo by Asahel Curtis, courtesy Washington State Historical Society*

*Mountain Goat Planted in Olympic National Forest in 1925. Photo by Chris Morgenroth, courtesy of Kathrine Morgenroth, Flaherty Collection*

*Fire Prevention, Olympia, Washington, ca. 1919. Special Collections, University of Washington*

Higley, Hank Vallad, and Packer Ernest Vorhees worked the skyline trail. J. Denny Ahl was at Hoodsport assisting the durable Ralph Hilligoss.

Clarence Adams recorded the following:

*In August, 1917, Harold A. Browning, Francis S. Fuller, O.K. Roberts, William Danz, Ralph Krojewski and H. E. Sallee were drafted into the Army for World War I from the Olympic.*

*During the summer of 1917, E. J. Hanzlik, then Forest Examiner, started the first semi-extensive timber survey in Region 6 on the South Skokomish not hitherto tried on a large scale. This job was intermediate in character between intensive timber surveys and our old extensive reconnaissance. [sic]*

Hanzlik himself later reminisced:

*From 1914-1918 I was in charge of timber surveys and mapping; also worked on timber sales, lands, and other activities. Headquarters at Olympia, first in the Funk-Volland Bldg. on Capital Way (Main St.) and 5th Avenue; then in Post Office Building. Was fortunate to be on the Olympic in the so-called old days when it took "he-men" foresters to do the job—covering the forest on foot, mostly back–packing supplies, and being real pioneers in the forestry movement and in forestry practice. [sic]*

Chris Morgenroth, who embodied the popular epitome of the early Forest Ranger, had been treed by wolves, completed an elk population study and was the organizing genius behind getting the trails opened up after the big blowdown of "21." Chris was always eager to try new and innovative ideas. In 1924, he persuaded Supervisor Fromme to allow him passage as an aerial observer on the Penny Creek Fire. The army pilot and Chris crashed on the ridge about two miles above the Corrigenda Guard Station. Clarence Adams, with his clerical pen recalls:

*During the summer of 1924, while I was on the Penny Creek Fire (Quilcene Ranger District), an Army pilot with former District Ranger Morgenroth as observer flew over the Olympic and crashed on the ridge about two miles above Corrigenda Guard Station. With a helper, I took a pickup from Quilcene and brought both men into Quilcene where we met a physician who had been called in from Port Townsend. We used two rooms in the Quilcene Hotel as a hospital and surgery. The doctor performed the operation on Chris and I administered the anesthetic. Chris' face was badly torn from both corners of his mouth down to the lower part of his chin and the Pilot had several teeth knocked out.*

Of his many adventures and accomplishments, perhaps the most lasting is Morgenroth's penchant for planting flowers and shrubs, like a forester's green version of Johnny

Appleseed. An Olympic mountain lake bears the Morgenroth name in grateful tribute to the man and the legend.

Perhaps the most interesting and ironic anecdote concerning Morgenroth was the January 1, 1925, incident witnessed by the ever-present Clarence Adams who by now was given the title of Administrative Assistant:

> *Chris and I turned two pair of mountain goats loose on Highway 101 near the Storm King Ranger Station. Chris didn't think of what might happen when they were unloaded, so he just stood there waiting to see what they would do. I was near the truck door and the door was open. One of the real he goats looked at Chris, sized him up, and then with his head down, bolted for him and Chris being near an old snag, reached as high as he could and pulled himself up just out of reach of the ram's butt. [sic]*

The introduction of the mountain goat was a planned joint venture of the Olympic National Forest, E. B. Webster of the Klahane Club, Clallam County Sheriff and Game Warden, Jack Pike, and members of the State Game Commission. A subsequent exchange in 1929 of Alaska goats for Roosevelt elk, raised by the Huelsdonk sisters on their Hoh River Ranch, resulted in an influx of animals which thrived in their new habitat.

Chris Morgenroth abruptly resigned from the Forest Service when a change of administration occurred in the Portland Regional Office. That same year, 1926, found Rudo Fromme being transferred to the Deschutes National Forest. Attempts to link Fromme with a land investment scheme proved false and he was completely exonerated. His departure from the Olympic elicited the following editorial in the *Port Angeles Evening News*:

> *Monday, March 29, 1926*
>
> *R. L. FROMME HAS BEEN MOVED TO PORTLAND FORESTRY OFFICE*
>
> *R. L. Fromme, Olympic forest supervisor, who wrote "Oh Olympia, Highway to the Olympics," and who has endeared himself to practically everyone in Washington state by his friendliness, his capable management of forest affairs and his penchant for keeping the public friendly and informed of forest happenings has been taken from Olympia and put into the Portland office. [sic]*
>
> *Rumblings of the change were on for a month. Then it was announced a man from the Deschutes National Forest would succeed him.*
>
> *Clallam County will miss Fromme. He is a type of supervisor of which the service may well be proud. If he has a fault it is that of not wanting to be tangled up in governmental tape. Fromme believes that when a forest is on fire the sensible thing is to put it out, not phone for orders.*
>
> *As a result of co-operation by local foresters, Mr. Fromme and this paper, fire prevention education has been carried on with good results here. Fromme's vision saw necessity for the Elwha road when others*

*frowned on it. His co-operation was responsible for the road to Ovington's which will be completed this summer. His foresight had the Seven Lakes Basin road put in the road plan of the forestry service.*

*Fromme was so well liked in his official capacity that he was able to ask and receive more co-operation than any like officer could reasonably expect.*

*Supervisor Plum, who succeeds Mr. Fromme is a fine gentlemen and we will welcome him here and extend the right hand of co-operation. Just the same we'll miss Fromme. We lose, Portland wins. [sic]*

Rudo Fromme was honored by the Seattle Mountaineers who named an Olympic Peak for him. Fromme himself named many geographical land marks in the Olympics. One significant name change was made to honor Forest Ranger Roy Muncaster of Quinault who lost his life, his vessel torpedoed en route to France in World War I.

Bill Bryan worked three summers on the Olympic beginning in 1920 at the Salonie Guard Station on the Quinault District. He reminisced about some of those early days in a letter to the regional forester:

*After a winter at school, I returned to work in late May, 1921. A wind storm the previous February had caused heavy blowdown extending from Quinault along the coast to near Lake Crescent. A special appropriation of about $300,000 had been provided for extra protection on this area of high fire hazard. Snider Ranger Station, designated as headquarters for the increased protection force and equipment, was a beehive of building activity, where only a shake cabin had stood before. I arrived there in late May. Oliver Erickson, assistant supervisor was in charge. The District headquarters were in Port Angeles, Chris Morgenroth, District Ranger.*

*A few days later I moved to Forks and the Peterson ranch as fire dispatcher. The Army Air Corps of Fort Lewis contracted to fly a daily patrol. Planes were equipped with radio to be used in reporting fires as soon as spotted. A receiving set was installed and manned by the Army Signal Corps at the Peterson ranch. The Peterson ranch was selected because it had the only cow pasture suitable for a landing field. The dispatcher, with Forest Service phone lines to the Hoh, Bogachiel and Snider, received reports of fires from the army operator and sent them on to the appropriate guard or crew. The set-up didn't work, mainly because radio equipment was quite crude in those days, especially transmission from the plane. At the end of June, Supervisor Fromme asked me how I liked the job. I didn't like it, and a few days later I was en route to Hoodsport to help Dennie Ahl on phone line maintenance. Ralph Hilligoss was ranger at Hoodsport. The season ended back at Salonie. David C. Hartsuck was ranger and Fred Briem district assistant. Hartsuck had succeeded Roy Muncaster, killed in World War I. [sic]*

In the fall of 1922, Bryan passed the ranger examination and was appointed timber sale officer at Quinault and acted as district ranger until Joe Fulton was transferred from Quilcene. Bryan's letter continues:

*The principal sale during the winter was the Furness sale on Canoe Creek. This was a selective cut sale of sorts, since only the most decadent cedar was marked for cutting, yarded by horses and towed to the Bailey Mill located at the lower end of Lake Quinault near the site of the present Indian Service headquarters. Travel to the sale area was by Forest Service boat. The boat, formerly a Captain's gig with service in the Canadian navy, proved unwieldy for a single oarsman. To off-set this, the District had purchased an outboard motor, possibly the first motor built by Evinrude. A typical lake crossing started with thirty minutes or more in attempting to start the motor, finally resigned to rowing with pauses for further goes at the motor with success usually attained a few hundred feet short of the opposite shore. The homeward voyage was frequently a repeat performance.*

I was transferred to Quilcene about August 1 as District Ranger. Bill Vallad was D. A. Headquarters were at Fulton's former residence at the head of Quilcene Bay and consisted of a small corrugated iron building with desk in one corner and the rest of the space devoted to equipment storage. Part of this building is now used as the Quilcene Ranger Station oil house. The District extended from the Duckabush to Deer Park.

The one sale on the district was the Snow Creek Logging Company sale which covered most of the Snow Creek Drainage. The sale started about 1917 and terminated in 1925. stumpage was $1.50 for Douglas-fir and $.50 for hemlock. Fir was later raised to $1.75 over protests by George Webb, president of the company. Sales of this period were usually large and cruised and appraised by the Regional office. The TSO's were project men responsible to the Supervisor officer at Snow Creek, but resigned at termination of the sale.

Earl McArdle was TSO on the Webb Logging Company sale, which included the Fulton and Waketich Creek drainage, until 1926 when he resigned. He was later re-employed as superintendent of the Snider C.C.C. camp. McArdle was followed by L.D. Blodgett. Webb cut out in 1929 and Blodgett took over the C. B. & M. sale in the Mt. Turner-Rocky Brook area and the Hamma Hamma logging Company sale during the 1927 to about 1933 period. This period was marked by increased emphasis on utilization and fire protection.

*Ranger Hilligoss (left)*

Dennie Ahl, one of the regions top scalers, Pete Wyss, Otto Lindh, Paul Logan, and Al Tyler were scalers along the Canal at that time. [sic]

*Olympic Aerial Squadron, 1921*

*Flying Fire Patrol (1921–1922)*

*Airplane Crash in the Olympics,*
*Chris Morgenroth, 1924.*
*Special Collections, University of Washington*

*Ranger Meeting, Tacoma, Washington, (Rainier and Olympic) March 1923. Left to right: back row, Chris Morgenroth, William Sethe, Jules Hagon (died Sept. 19, 1927), Arnold Arneson, Harry Croxford; middle row, R.L. Fromme, E.J. Fenby, F.E. Ames, A.O. Vaka, J.H. Billingslea, A.A. Griffin (died Oct, 28, 1924), J.W. Fulton, R.A. Hilligoss; front row, G.G. Allen (died Aug. 16, 1924), G.E. Griffith, E.W. Kavanagh, Jno.D. Guthrie, W.D. Byran, John Kirkpatrick*

*Ranger Harstuck With Family and Friends Visiting and Enjoying a Meal With the Finley Peak Lookout. Courtesy of Carolyn Wright, Daughter of Ranger Hartsuck.*

*The ranger is the man on the ground. He lives there. He is in the position to see the effects of our work at all seasons and under all circumstances, and it is these effects, and nothing else, that counts. His is the task of applying our principles in detail, and it is not until they are applied in detail that they have any effects.*

*Aldo Leopold*

The Olympic was fortunate in many ways in 1927: Sanford Floe was chosen to replace the legendary Morgenroth and John Ray Bruckart was assigned as the Assistant Supervisor. Both men were true role models of the ranger concepts described so aptly by Aldo Leopold. Active and aggressive, they were destined to serve the Olympic well during the heart of the Great Depression which affected all Americans in the cities, farms, and forests.

Sanford "Sandy" Floe received permission to live, and establish the District office, at Snider Ranger Station. Years later, "Sandy" recalled some of his early days in a letter to the regional forester, J. Herbert Stone:

> *The Port Angeles Ranger District covered the area from Deer Park West and South to the divide between the Hoh and Queets River, about 660,500 acres.*
>
> *There was about 200 miles of trail on the district, mostly in the main drainages. No Forest Service roads. A county road from the Olympic Highway at Fairholm Hill to Soleduck Hot Springs. Clallam County and the Forest Service cooperated during 1927 to 1929 in building the road from Rica Canyon Dam to the Olymp Hot Springs. The Northwestern Power & Light, a Washington Pulp subsidiary, was building the Rica Canyon Dam.*
>
> *There were no Forest Service pack strings. The servicing of the back country guard stations, lookouts and trail crews was a problem. I had brought four horses from Oregon with me but that number was inadequate. There were a few local farmers with pack animals of poor quality but they were usually packing tourist parties when we needed them. In the spring of 1928, Supervisor Plumb sent J.R. Bruckart to Yakima to buy some mules.*
>
> *The Soleduck Valley was mostly uncut. Bloedel-Donovan had established the Sappho Camp about 1925 and started cutting on the Clallam Lumber Company holdings. In 1927 the Irving-Hartley (Later the Crescent Logging Company) established the "Riverside" camp across the Soleduck from Snider Ranger Station. Bloedel-Donovan put a logging camp at what is now known as "Cooper's Ranch". The combined cut of these three large railroad logging outfits was about 500 million a year for the next several years, all shipped to upsound mills as there were no sawmills operating in Port Angeles. [sic]*

*Ranger Sanford Floe, Prickett, George Drake, Fred Cleator at Snider Ranger Station, 1927*

Early in 1919 the North Pacific District of the Forest Service, headquartered in Portland, created a recreation division and put Fred W. Cleator, former Deputy Forest Supervisor of the Colville National Forest in eastern Washington, in charge. The name of his office was broadened to "Land Classification" in 1921 and to "Lands" in 1922.

Fred Cleator, in his role as recreation examiner for Region 6, made a field study of the Olympic National Forest and Mt. Olympus National Monument. His recommendations resulted in a comprehensive management guide for all recreational use. This comprehensive analysis is referred to as the Cleator Plan and was a model for Pacific Northwest recreational planning and development. In accordance with Forest Service policy, various forms of recreation were encouraged: public campgrounds, resorts, summer homes, organization/group building sites and winter sports areas such as the complex at Deer Park. The demand and appreciation for outdoor recreation experiences intensified on the peninsula with the expansion of the road system that culminated with the completion of the loop highway in 1931. Private interests became involved in commercial ventures within the remote national forest interior. The Olympic Chalet Company was organized to promote the recreational opportunities in the Olympic Mountains and make them available to the public. Special use permits were issued for a backcountry, rustic chalet at Low Divide and a shelter at the halfway point from Lake Quinault. Other speculative recreational facilities were proposed such as an airport landing strip, a dammed alpine lake for hydroplanes, and an aerial tramway to the top of Mt. Baldy for a ski

*Snider Fire Patrol, Prickett and Drake (in Hat), 1927*

*Registry Booth at Snider Camp Ground—Ranger Sanford Floe is Issuing Fire Permit, September 1927*

*A One-Cylinder Reo on the Port Angeles Road. Reo cars were sold between 1906 and 1936. Courtesy Bert Kellogg*

facility. None of these proposals were realized but they did indicate the concerted efforts by Grays Harbor citizens to foster tourism and recreational growth for the peninsula.

"Qui Si Sana"

Sanatorium and Biological Institution

Lake Crescent, Washington

PIEDMONT POST OFFICE

DR. LOUIS DECHMANN, Proprietor

TREATMENTS will be given patients suffering of Anaemia, Diabetes Mellitus, Bright's Disease, Obesity, Rheumatism and Gout, Neurasthenia in most forms, Diseases peculiar to Women, Impotence and Sterility.

COMFORTABLE HOTEL ACCOMMODATIONS
HOT SPRINGS AND MINERAL SPRINGS IN
IMMEDIATE VICINITY

For further information write to
Dr. Louis Dechmann
City Residence: 127 North Fifty-Ninth Street
Seattle, Washington, U.S.A.

"Qui Si Sana" [illegible]

*One Page From a Promotional Brochure of the 1920 Era*

The regional forester on April 15, 1922, enhanced the protection of public recreation values by formally dedicating a territory of 6,621 acres surrounding Quinault Lake as a Recreation Area. This included the Natural Area which had been examined earlier and documented by the veteran woodsman and renowned silviculturist, Leo Isaac.

A Primitive Area of 134,240 acres was created by the chief forester on December 22, 1930. Later, the secretary of agriculture revised and enlarged the area to 238,930 acres, which included 2,544,480 board feet of merchantable timber. This reservation was administered to preserve vast stands of old-growth Douglas-fir, cedar, and other tree species indigenous to

*"Qui si sana" Popular Resort/ Spa Owner, Dr. Dechman, Lake Crescent, ca. 1924*

*Falls Creek Campground, Lake Quinault, 1926*

the Olympic Peninsula. It also created sufficient pristine area to provide rugged individuals the recreational opportunity to commune with nature, undisturbed by the turmoil and confusion of civilization.

The pioneer Olson family was active in all facets of Quinault community life. As in most families who settled on the peninsula, their lives were intertwined with the Forest Service. The large Olson clan was known for their personal concern toward their neighbors and their open hospitality that often characterized the friendliness of the frontier. J. A. Olson, the patriarch of the family, raised domesticated elk, as did the Huelsdonk family who homesteaded on the Hoh and Bogachiel rivers. Five of the Olson brothers competed with the Olympic Chalet Company when they organized a guide service for hikers and campers in 1926. They formed the Olympic Recreation Company and applied for permission from the Forest Service to develop three recreational sites in the east fork drainage of the Quinault. The Graves Creek Inn and a chalet, located in the "Valley Of A Thousand Waterfalls" as it was popularly known by the locals, were actually constructed.

Fred Cleator, the recreation engineer for Region 6, suggested to the Olsons that the area be called "Enchanted Valley." This name and the chalet survive today due to restoration efforts of the Grays Harbor Olympians Hiking Club, and others, with the cooperation and management of the National Park Service.

Mavie Olson was the Finley Peak lookout in the early days; her twin sisters Nellie and Sellie married Forest Ranger Bill Vallad, and Doug Osborn, respectively. Doug claimed to be the first "cat skinner" on the Olympic while he was employed by Frank Ritter, the forest engineer at the time. Doug worked on forest fires and helped build roads in the Deer Park and Elwha areas from 1927 until 1934 when he went into the logging business. Doug Osborn recalled "walking his cat" from the north shore of Lake Quinault to Clallam Bay: "this was before the Loop Highway was finished. It took me three days and they were twelve hour days." Doug's brother, Wallace, worked on trails in the 1920s and 1930s and sister-in-law, Agnes, clerked at the Quinault

*Olympic Highway, Eastern Terminus, May 1925*

Ranger Station. As a small child, Chester Wilson rode into the Quinault Valley with the Olson family from Minnesota, which included Chester's mother and Mrs. J. A. Olson, who were sisters. Chester worked on the trail crew with Ranger E. R. Paull. Chester and his cousin, "Fritz" Olson, were also employed at the West Fork Splash Dam which was owned by the Humptulips Driving Company. Chester Creek and Chester Ridge were named for Chester Wilson.

In keeping with early day Forest Service policy at the time, commercial interests and developments were encouraged. In 1910, the owner/operator of Olympic Hot Springs was issued a special use permit to pipe mineral water to the city of Port Angeles. Various improvements were made in the 20s, and in 1930, a road to the hot springs was completed through the cooperative effort of the Olympic National Forest and Clallam County. The Hot Springs Resort complex and other recreational facilities such as the Deer Park Ski Area, Lake Cushman, Lake Crescent and Lake Quinault were modified, altered or eliminated when jurisdiction was transferred to the National Park Service.

John (Jack) Schwartz began his Olympic National Forest career in the spring of 1930 on a tree-planting crew. His seasonal employment also included preliminary trail reconnaissance on the Hoodsport District that was supervised by Ranger Hilligoss. On the 12th of July that year, they experienced the worst lightning bust on the Olympic. Jack Schwartz and Bruce Ritter were responsible for moving fire crews up Lake Cushman. All districts were affected by the electrical storm and were occupied fighting fires throughout the entire summer. As a result of the 1929-1930 fire seasons, more lookouts were constructed to improve the fire detection and protection system.

Prior to 1940, the list of lookouts on the Olympic included:

Finley Peak (1916)
Kloshe Nanitch (1917)
Sol Duc (1919)
Deer Park (1928)
Big Quilcene (1930)
Mt. Constance (1930)
Colonel Bob (1933)
Dodger Point (1933)
Hurricane Ridge (1933)
Ned Hill (1933)
Mt. Townsend (1933)
Higley Peak (1933)
Webb Mountain (1934)
Anderson Butte (1937)
North Point (1939)

The impact of the 1929 collapse of the American economy was immense in all sections of the country and felt by all social classes. The severity of the situation called for bold, dramatic and drastic measures. As part of a national recovery plan, the Civilian Conservation Corps was formed with a mandate to alleviate problems related to the use and conservation of natural resources.

In the spring of 1934, J. R. Bruckart was detailed to the regional office in Portland to assist the division of engineering with the overall supervision of the CCC program. His memoirs offer insight into this revolutionary social program:

> *Work projects were initiated by the Forest Service and responsibility for supervision of the CCC work crews was the responsibility of Forest Service supervisory personnel. Ordinarily this consisted of a Camp Superintendent and of a 200-man company of four to six foremen. Also several enrollees were designated as straw bosses or assistant foremen. Most of the Forest Service facilitating personnel were selected from regular Forest Service personnel and local experienced logging and private construction supervisory people...*
>
> *...A great many worthwhile projects were accomplished by the Civilian Conservation Corps during its eight years of existence. After 1940 unemployment declined and it became increasingly difficult to get young men to enlist in the Corps. Finally the program was abolished, but in the meantime many thousands of young men who might never had the opportunity learned useful skills and had the experience of working in the forests as useful citizens. [sic]*

Political ramifications in the CCC program soon surfaced and Bruckart was able to put them in proper perspective:

> *During the short period that I was assigned to the Regional Office, I had the opportunity to work closely with Regional Forester C. J. Buck on problems relating to the selection of supervisory personnel for the CCC camps. At the time the program started, the Forest Service had a free hand in the selection of supervisory personnel for the camps. After the program had been in operation for several months, state and county political organizations became aware that these were pretty well paid jobs. In the CCC program, the same pressures developed among some congressmen and when openings occured, (they requested the Forest Service) fill the positions with men they recommended. The Forest Service had no choice but (to abide by these requests). However, some members of the congressional delegation from Washington complained that the Regional Forester, Mr. Buck, was not cooperating in placing the men they recommended for the CCC supervisory jobs.*
>
> *In an effort to explain to the congressmen his position in selecting supervisory personnel and his desire to cooperate with them, Mr. Buck decided to make a swing through the State of Washington to contact members of the Washington delegation. This (was in) the fall of 1935 and he requested that I accompany him because of my knowledge of the CCC program and the selection of the supervisory personnel. Our interviews with the congressmen and one senator were quite friendly and most were reasonably satisfied. [sic]*

On November 1, 1935, when J. R. Bruckart returned to the Olympic as Forest Supervisor, the following were year-long personnel:

L. L. Colville, Assistant Forest Supervisor; E. J. Hanzlik, Associate Forester; Paul H. Logan, Lumberman; Arthur E. Glover, Associate Engineer; L. D. Blodgett, Ranger (timber sales); Christian N. Skaar, Ranger Staff; Clarence Adams, Administrative Assistant; Julia Lee and Helen Engel, Clerks. District Rangers were Port Angeles District, Sanford Floe, W. D. Bryan, Assistant; Elwha District, Le Roy Olander; Quilcene District, M. J. Mapes, J. R. Blake, Assistant; Hoodsport District, John Hough; Quinault District, J. W. Fulton; Simpson Logging Company Sale, Ralph Hilligoss and Denny Ahl.

All of the full-time rangers on the Olympic were involved as liaison between the Army and CCC field projects.

*Seattle Mountaineers Outing, Finley Peak Lookout, 1920, Mavie Olson (foreground), Professor Edmond Meany (front row). Special Collections Division, University of Washington Libraries, negative no. UW12942*

*Geyser Valley House on the Elwha, Doc Ludden (left) With Klahane Club Hikers, E. B. Webster Seated (right), 1926*

Chester Wilson. Courtesy Raleigh Wilson

"In the Field" Left to right: Oscar Peterson, Packer; Mrs. Floe, Ranger Sanford Floe, Mrs. Plumb, Forest Supervisor H.L. Plumb, unidentified

Domesticated Elk, John Olson Ranch, Lake Quinault Valley. Courtesy Doug Osborn

Olympic Hot Springs Resort, 1930. Courtesy Klahane Club

*Klahane Lodge, Mountaineers From Port Angeles*

*J. B. Wattinger, Carrie Wattinger, Mrs. Chris Morgenroth*

*Humptulips Driving Company*
*Courtesy Raleigh Wilson*

*Low Divide Chalet Under Construction, 1927*

*Logging the Homestead Claim, Ernest Olson, Quinault. Courtesy May Torres*

*Ranger Ralph Hilligoss, Hoodsport, Issuing Campfire Permit, ca. 1926*

*The Forks to Clallam Bay Road Under Construction, ca. 1917. A Velie Truck is Being Loaded With Gravel at the Right. At the Top of the Photograph is a Donkey Engine Used to Pull Gravel Up the Ramp of the Bunker. Courtesy Bert Kellogg*

*Finley Peak Lookout, First Lookout on the Olympic (Constructed in 1916)*

*Low Divide Chalet From South Side of Meadow, Parts of Mt. Seattle in Background, 1927*

*North Point Lookout "Slick" Hiles, "Dutch" Holt Husen, ca. 1941. Courtesy Robert Hardy*

*Spring Boards on the West Fork Humptulips, Chester Wilson (right) Courtesy Raleigh Wilson*

*Finley Peak Lookout*

*Webb Lookout Under Construction, Quilcene Ranger District, Built by Ralph McClanahan*

*Mt. Townsend Lookout, Lean-to Shed for Mules in Foreground, 1935*

*Dodger Point Lookout, 1933*

*Hyas Lookout, Sol Duc Ranger District, J.R. (Jack) Rooney Lookout/Fireman, 1953*

*Bud Hopkins Operating the Osborne Firefinder, Hurricane Ridge Lookout, July 4, 1938*

*Colonel Bob Lookout, Quinault District, Harold Deery, ca. 1939. Courtesy Harold Deery*

*Enjoying the View. Left to right: Forest Supervisor John R. Bruckart, Les Colville, Paul Logan, Engineer Glover, Elwah Ranger LeRoy Olander*

*Blyn Lookout, Built by CCC's, 1933*

*Harold White Plotting a Smoke, Webb Lookout Station*

*Enchanted Valley Chalet, Olympic Recreation Company (Constructed Under Special Permit Issued by U.S. Forest Service). Asahel Curtis Collection, Washington State Historical Society*

*Anderson Butte Lookout, Shelton Ranger District, Wally Wheeler on Trail, July 8, 1952*

*"Visiting Hours" Clarence Adams (left) Sellie and Nellie Olson (center), ca. 1918. Courtesy Doug Osborn*

*C. J. Buck, Regional Forester; Thornton T. Munger; Chester Morse (Region 5); Mr. Fechner, Director of the CCC; J. R. Bruckart, Supervisor; Silcox, Chief Forester; James Franklin and Ranger John Kirkpatrick. Taken on Columbia National Forest, August, 1934*

*Rangers and Their Rigs. Left to right: District Rangers Monte J. Mapes, Quilcene; Sanford M. Floe, Sol Duc; Joe Fulton, Quinault; L.D. Blodgett, Port Angeles; Waldemar Anderson, Hoodsport; Forest Supervisor J.R. Bruckart*

*Forest Guard School Instructors, Louella Guard Station, Quilcene District, 1937. First row: Jack Fay; Glover, Forest Engineer; J.R. Bruckart, Forest Supervisor; Mealy, Sanford Floe, Snider District Ranger; Les Colville, Assistant Forest Supervisor; second row Roy Olander; L.D. Blodgett, Port Angeles District Ranger; Anderson; Jack Schwartz, Wildlife Biologist; Joe Fulton, Quinault District Ranger; Howard Johnson, Quilcene District; Cory; Bill Bryan, Quilcene District Ranger; Hough*

*Fire Protective Force, Quinault–Port Angeles; Joe Kestner (2nd row, 4th from right) Howard "Bo" Elder (2nd row, 3rd from right), ca. 1938*

*"Eagle's Aerie" Spar Tree Lookout, Cook Creek, Constructed 1929*

*Idle through no fault of your own, you were enrolled from city and rural homes and offered an opportunity to engage in healthful, outdoor work on forest, park and soil conservation projects of definite practical value to all the people of the nation. The promptness with which you seized the opportunity to engage in honest work, the willingness with which you have performed your daily tasks and the fine spirit you have shown in winning the respect of the communities in which your camps have been located, merits the admiration of the entire country. You, and the men who have guided and supervised your efforts, have cause to be proud of the record the CCC has made in the development of sturdy manhood and in the initiation and prosecution of a conservation program of unprecedented proportions...*

> *Excerpts from a message from the President of the United States to members of the CCC read over NBC network at 7:30 p.m., Friday, April 17, 1936.*

The Olympic National Forest was the beneficiary of many CCC programs with the establishment of camps and side camps under the jurisdiction of the Fort Lewis District. A list of the Forest Camps and their accomplishments is well documented in the official annual published in 1937. Historical excerpts give a glimpse into stark reality of the Depression Era:

*"Early in the life of the Civilian Conservation Corps there was formed one of the first companies to enter the Olympic National Forest. The camp to be occupied was F-21, Quinault, Washington, the number of the company was 982. A cadre of twenty-five men reached the camp site on May 21, 1933, and, under the direction of Lieut. William Long, Regular Army, with the assistance of three Regular Army Sergeants, a tent camp was set up. One week later 200 recruits from local counties joined the advanced guard. From the beginning Company 982 was destined to make history and records to be pointed to with pride. Every month of the company's short stay at F-21 they topped the accomplishment list of the five camps in the Olympic National Forest on the work project. On October 13, 1933, the address of*

*CCC Camp Quinault, Norwood Ranger Station Site. Special Collections Division, University of Washington Libraries, photo by Clark Kinsey, negative no. UW10689*

*CAMP QUINAULT, WASHINGTON, F-21*

*Part of Camp F-21, Quinault River. Photo by K. D. Swan, August 1933*

*Enrollee Leo Mayo at Humptulips Side Camp. Photo by Robert Hardy*

*CCC Boys Busy Saturday Afternoon, Washing Their Clothes, Quinault Camp. Photo by Albert Wiesendanger, August 1933*

*CCC Humptulips Side Camp. Photo by Robert Hardy*

*Recreation Tent at Quinault CCC Camp. Photo by K. D. Swan, September 1933*

*the company changed to Elma, Washington, where they moved into permanent Camp P-208, located one mile east of the town of Elma..." [sic]*

*"On Tuesday, May 16, 1933, orders were received at Fort Worden for the occupation of a camp site near Quilcene, Washington. A group had been assembled at Fort Worden, located on the northeast point of the Olympic Peninsula, for conditioning and organization. From this group Company 946 was formed." [sic]*

*"The following morning an advance party of twenty-five enrollees, with Capt. F. L. Topping, Commanding, proceeded to Quilcene, twenty-five miles south of Fort Worden. They were met by Ranger M. J. Mapes, who led them to the Forest Service campsite three miles south of Quilcene on the north side of Penny Creek near a point where it joins the Big Quilcene River. A meal was prepared with the equipment and provisions supplied by the Quartermaster at Fort Worden. Then everyone pitched in to set up a temporary tent camp." [sic]*

*"During the winter of 1935- 1936, a new recreation hall was added, new shops and more equipment were provided. Several big road construction and building projects were going. Side camps were maintained at Corregenda and Louella..." [sic]*

*"In June, 1936, the scenic Mount Walker Road was completed. Big dedication, big crowds, big feathers in the CCC boys' caps. [sic] "After the big Oregon fire was whipped in October, the Quilcene CCC changed to the Quilcene FFF-'Fire Fightin' Fools. [sic]*

*"In March, 1937, Camp Quilcene was judged the leading camp in the U.S. in vocational education and training by officials from Washington D.C. [sic]*

*"November 5, 1937, the first million trees had been planted. At this time, a few of the outstanding accomplishments that the men from Quilcene had done: 1,000,000 trees planted; 2,500 man-days fire fighting; 3,000 man-days fire hazard reduction; 4,300 signs, markers, seats, benches, tables, and other pieces of furniture had been made in the carpenter and sign shops; 55 miles of roads built; 20 miles of trails; 24 bridges built; 56 buildings constructed-the last one a 60x120 machine shops; 32 miles telephone line constructed; 17 campgrounds developed; 478 miles telephone lines maintained; 760 miles road maintained." [sic]*

Experienced men like Ralph McClanahan were the backbone for the success of Roosevelt's "Tree Army." His leadership and practical woodsmanship typified the technical support provided by the Forest Service. Howard Johnson, Charles McClanahan, Jack Schwartz, Lew Evans, Les Larson, Clarence Edgington, Walt Peterson, Ralph Reite, George Ohmert, Rollin Shaw, Robert Hardy, Tony Bogachis and Robert Bulchis were

*LASTING MONUMENTS BUILT BY THE CCC'S*

*Raising Bridge—Bent on Truck-Trail Up Quinault River, Boy From Camp F-21. Photo by K. D. Swan, August 1933*

*Quinault Side Camp Co. 938 Quinault River. Special Collections Division, University of Washington Libraries, photo by Clark Kinsey, negative no. 10687*

*Ranger Bill Vallad and Les Colville, Falls Creek Campground Community Kitchen, Built by CCC's, ca. 1935*

*Ranger Bill Vallad, Falls Creek Campground, ca. 1938*

involved with the Olympic CCC Camps and were able to utilize their experiences to further their Forest Service careers. For many enrollees, it proved to be a stabilizing influence in a precarious world where economic order had become chaos.

Robert Bulchis reminisced about his CCC days at Camp Louella where he was transferred in the fall of 1933:

> *Camp Louella at that time was in a raw state and the gumbo mud at the site was a conspicuous factor in the life there. To minimize the mud's nuisance, boardwalks were constructed connecting all the buildings. I was engaged primarily in construction of the Gold Creek Road. The foreman on this project was Walt Peterson. We felled trees and cleared the right of way. An important aspect of our work was the construction of numerous culverts using the red cedar trees growing abundantly in and near the right of way. I also did some patrol work for Monte Mapes, the Quilcene District Ranger, while an enrollee, mostly on the Gold Creek Trail. Beyond the end of the newly constructed road. One aspect of CCC life I remember were the efforts to provide simple educational courses. The instructor in one of these, another Enrollee, provided the impetus which eventually led to my attending the U of W Forestry School. One prominent individual who came in as a replacement enrollee at that time was Rodney Waldron, later Director of the Library at Oregon State University. [sic]*

Ranger Monte Mapes hired Robert Bulchis as lookout in 1935, 1936, and 1937. The 1935 season on Mt. Townsend lookout was memorable because Will Osborne, the inventor of the Fire Finder which bears his name, visited and personally took panoramic photos as part of a Regional Fire Prevention Project. Bulchis recalled the Green Mt.

*CCC Camp Quilcene, 1939*

*CAMP QUILCENE AND LOUELLA, WASHINGTON, F-19*

*Fish Pond Constructed by CCC's (Camp F-19) at Quilcene Federal Hatchery*

*Quilcene District CCC Foreman Ralph McClanahan and Crew Building a Bridge, 1933*

*Camp Quilcene Float, First Prize Winner, Port Angeles 4th of July Parade, 1936. Forest Service photo by Mortiboy*

*Railroad Trestle Built by CCC's*

*CCC Camp Quilcene Drum and Bugle Corps*

*Josephine Lee McCreery "Sweetheart of the CCC's."*
*Photo Courtesy of Jefferson County Historical Society*

*CCC's Tree Planters, Camp Quilcene*

*Robert Bulchis First Radioman on Olympic Fire*

Fire of 1938 when he was the first radio man on a forest fire on the Olympic:

*This was one of the bad fire years in the late 1930's. The season began at Quilcene in early June before many of the Guards had reported for work with a reburn of Green Mt. Don't recall too much about the height of the fire, but after it's peak, much of the mopping up operations were conducted from a camp called Airplane Camp atop the mountain that portion I believe called Mule Peak. We had several days of cloudiness which helped put it out.*

*This was the time when short wave radio communication was developed. I manned an SPF set on top of the mountain trying to direct a plane to drop supplies for the camp being developed. This effort failed because of the dense fog and clouds. By the time the clouds cleared, a fire crew built a trail up the south side of the mountain from Townsend Creek until the first pack train arrived. The fog hampered mopping up operations initially because of the difficulty of sighting hot spots and keeping track of the work crews. Mopping up operations continued well into July. I was a straw boss on mopping up. [sic]*

Bulchis was nostalgic about his time as a seasonal employee on the Olympic and was able through words and photos to share his thoughts and memories with retired Quilcene Ranger, Robert Haase:

*Inspection Time, Ranger Monte Mapes (far right) CCC Foreman Ralph McClanahan (2nd from right) and CCC Crew Building Bridge, 1933*

*Camp Quilcene (CCC) Chow Line at Mess Hall*

*JIM BETHEL — Worked as a Guard a few years in Quilcene District. Jim, until recently, was Dean of the School of Forestry at the U of W for a number of years. In 1937, faceteously, I placed another arrow on the identification disk on Mt. Walker and pointed it toward a peak in the Iron Mt. area and named it Mt. Bethel. I doubt that the name stuck. [sic]*

*ROLLIN SHAW — Rollin was a long time resident who lived on a farm near Sequim. He was one of a group of local residents who was hired every year under the FS policy of reserving a certain number of summer jobs for local residents. As long as I can remember, he was the L.O. on Mt. Zion. Each year, Rollin would head for the mountain with his wife Daisy, three or four young sons, a herd of goats, et. al. to spend the summer. Daisy was like a mountain goat— would invariably out pace Rollin up the trail. She died about 1967. Rollin at last reports still lives near Sequim with an RFP PO address.*

*HOWARD JOHNSON — Howard was the man who did much of the supervision of U.S. Guards on the Quilcene District. Circumstances had forced Howard to leave college before he could get his Forestry degree. Each year, he received temporary renewable appointments until I believe the early 1940's when he was able to get converted to a permanent status under one of a number of Executive Orders which came into existence then. Howard went on to higher things in the Forest Service, retiring as Regional Forester of the Alaska Region about the mid 1970's.*

*TONY BOGACHUS — Tony still lives in Quilcene. I met Tony while fighting one of the fires in 1938. Somehow we learned that we were both of Lithuanian extraction. Not having spoken the language for a long time, we fought the fire vigorously while spouting Lithuanian to each other.*

*CCC Planting Crews at Work*

*Tree Planter, Robert Hardy. Photo by Robert Hardy*

*Tree Planter George "Turk" Ohmert. Photo by Robert Hardy*

*Howard Johnson (left) With Jack "Whiskers" Conrad on Winter Game Survey on Lost Mountain Road, 1937*

*CCC Building Shop*

*The Dosewallips River Road Under Construction by CCC's Near the Falls, Monte Mapes on Left. Photo by Robert Bulchis*

*Lawson Hopper, Joe Hazbrouck, Calvin "Fuzzie" Boyer, Bud Harlow, Gil McMasters. Photo by Robert Hardy*

*"Pals" (left to right) Lew Evans, Joe Morrison, Bud Hopkins, Ennis Creek Guard Station, ca. 1936. Photo by Robert Hardy*

*BILL GRAHAM — Bill was a school teacher who was dispatcher in the Quilcene District throughout the late 1930's, at least 1935 thru 1939. He died of a stroke in 1967--his last employment was as Personnel Director of Highline Community College in the Seattle area. His widow was Edna Graham, who spent every summer with Bill in Quilcene.*

*THE HARTS — Frank Hart and his wife ran the grocery store in Quilcene which we Forest Guards patronized in the 1930's. Frank is still living in Quilcene at age 93 and should have a storehouse of knowledge about Quilcene. His two sons Bob and Frank both worked as Forest Guards in the late 1930's and early 1940's. Bob went into engineering: Frank in Forestry at the U of W. [sic]*

Originally, the 938th Company was organized at Fort George Wright, Spokane, Washington, in May 1933. The unit was composed of ninety-eight men who were transferred to the Ft. Lewis District on October 23, 1933, where they immediately occupied Camp Twin which was under construction near Pysht.

*"During the winter of 1933-34, while at Camp Twin, the work of this company was entirely road building, and, in spite of an unusual amount of rain, a fine work record was established.*

*"In the spring of 1934, the company abandoned Camp Twin and occupied Camp Clearwater, on the western side of the Olympic Peninsula, in the rainiest section of*

*Camp F-20, at Cushman Lake. Photo by K D. Swan, August 1933*

*the United States. Under the direction of Camp Supt. Dan McGillicuddy, the men of the company constructed twenty-three miles of road and several fine bridges while at this location.*

*"In the fall of 1934, it was decided to keep the company at Clearwater for the winter and work was done to make the camp ready for winter. Steady rain was the fare until the 21st of January. When an unusually warm rain and wind caused the nearby Clearwater River to go over its banks and flood the camp. It was the worst flood ever experienced by the west end of the peninsula; all communications were cut off, roads were washed out, and for three days the camp was isolated. As the waters subsided, the men of the company rendered great aid to the civilian population in rehabilitation of the flooded area. [sic]*

*"After a pleasant summer at St. Andrews Creek, the company moved to Camp Canby, Ilwaco, Wash., for the winter of '35 and '36. Early in April orders were received that the company was to be disbanded and the men transferred to other companies in the District. April 22, the company was reorganized and the men previously transferred were recalled. The recently reorganized company immediately occupied Camp Lake Cushman, F-20, Hoodsport, Washington. [sic]*

*"The original company was organized at Fort Sheridan, Illinois, in 1933, and was sent to Camp Snider, F-16, located thirty-eight miles west of Port Angeles, Washington.*

*"Here the company built a good camp, felled snags on the well-known Sol Duc Burn, planted trees over the denuded mountains, constructed a road up the mountain, thinned trees, and fought various fires.*

*CAMP LAKE CUSHMAN, HOODSPORT, WASHINGTON, F-20*

*Making an Oar. Photo by K. D. Swan, August 1933*

*CCC Powder Monkeys, F-20 Camp Cushman*

*CCC Boys Building Boats From Split Cedar, Recreational Activity. Photo by K. D. Swan, August 1933*

*Road Construction, Lake Cushman. Photo by Ernest Lindsey U.S. Forest Service*

*"On April 30, 1934, the company moved to Camp Boulder, F-8, near Winthrop, Washington, where it made roads, constructed trails, and built a lookout station.*

*"From Boulder Company 1632 moved back to Snider, where it continued the projects formerly begun. There the following spring the number of the company was changed and it has since been known as Company 2916. Besides the work carried on at the main camp, the project was furthered by a side camp at Humptulips, and by one at the Hoh River Side Camp where a forest ranger station was constructed. [sic]*

*"In July, 1937, Company 2916 moved to Elwha, F-17, located on the Elwha River, at the foot of Hurricane Ridge, thirteen miles from Port Angeles, Washington. Since that date a great deal of effort has been put into the reconditioning of an old camp. Some men are constructing roads, some are improving the road to Olympic Hot Springs. Some are developing the winter resort at Deer Park. All feel their new home has a most beautiful location, and when the camp is fully reconditioned, it will be a very desirable place to live. Its location for educational, religious and recreational advantages is ideal.*

*"Enrollees, Gossar and Cochran, rescued two lost civilians from woods near Sol Duc Hot Springs. Crews fighting the Southern Oregon Fire and the Randall Fire in Washington received letters of appreciation for their efficient service under trying conditions." [sic]*

The Forest Service relinquished Camp Elwha to the jurisdiction of the National Park Service in December 1938. Cutbacks had been made nationwide by Mr. Fechner, Director of the CCC, due to budget constraints.

*Peeling Logs for CCC Building at Lake Cushman Camp, 1933*

In addition to the advent of the 1930s CCC program on the Olympic, several other historic events occurred which drastically altered the role and morale of the Olympic National Forest. In June 1933, administration of the Mt. Olympus National Monument was transferred to the National Park Service. The memoirs of J. R. Bruckart poignantly reveal his personal and emotional involvement associated with the fragmentation and transfer of stewardship of the National Forest.

*I was happy with my assignment to the Olympic, having spent about three years on the Forest as Assistant Forest Supervisor. However, I had not anticipated the controversy that was developing between the Forest Service and the National Park Service and their supporters over a proposal to create a National Park as set forth in a House of Representative bill introduced by Congressman Walgren. There was a National Monument in the central part of the Forest that included Mt. Olympus, that involved about 300,000 acres. The Monument was created in about 1906 primarily for the preservation of the large number of Roosevelt Elk that made their home in the Olympics. The Forest Service had always administered the land within the Monument until 1933 when all monuments on most public land were transferred to the National Park Service for administration. The Park Service immediately established a monument headquarters in Port Angeles. Preston Macy, a very personable Park Ranger from (the) Mt. Rainier National Park was placed in charge. Without doubt, his principal duties were to promote the support for the establishment of the proposed National Park... [sic]*

*As mentioned Congressman Walgren had proposed to create a national park in the Olympic to include the Monument and a few thousand acres around it. The policy of the Forest Service (opposition to the national park) was backed by Secretary of Agriculture, Henry Wallace. However, he was no match for Harold Ickes, the Secretary of the Interior (in the Roosevelt Administration). [sic]*

Key Forest Service employees during this transition period were Jack Schwartz and Sandy Floe. Jack Schwartz finished his college degree at the University of Washington and became one of four Forest Service Wildlife Biologists in the entire Pacific Northwest Region. The Olympic Elk Study was the result of a cooperative program between the U.S. Biological Survey and the Forest Service. This evolved as a comprehensive plan for elk and other wildlife resources of the Olympic National Forest. Activities included field surveys on the Hoh, Queets, and Quinault river drainages where the greatest concentrations of elk were found. Habitat conditions, feeding habits, general behavior, herd movements, population trends, and winter losses, were some of the elk management data that were collected and studied.

*Portal at Camp Elwha. Photo by K.D. Swan, August 1933*

Elk exclosures were constructed and maintained on a year-long basis to measure habitat conditions and grazing effects on elk habitat. Biologist Schwartz was assisted by George Ohmert who worked full time on the elk study. Three or four college students (wildlife majors) also assisted in the establishment and measurement of vegetative sample plots on the primary elk ranges. Ranger Sanford Floe reminisced about one of the dramatic events that occurred that autumn:

> *In October 1937 the Hoh Valley was opened to Elk hunting after some twenty years of closure. There was an estimated 2,000 people in the area. This was four or five times the number expected and created a "Coxey's Army" situation. Biologist Jack Schwartz, two experienced Guards and myself were the Forest Service people in the area. The State Game Department had five or six protectors there. [sic]*
>
> *The first night a former Forest Service employee visiting among the camps accidentally shot a hole in the gasoline lantern pressure tank in a tent. He and two others had to be hospitalized for burns. In rapid succession a hunter was shot and killed on the head of Owl Creek, miles from a road and it took the combined efforts of all Forest and Game Department people to get the body out. A party of hunters tried to ford the Hoh River in a truck, drowning one of them. A hunter shot himself in the leg about six miles out in the timber and his partners were so exhausted they could not guide us back to him. We did find him. Someone shot a white horse being used to pack out elk meat. Then we had four or five inches of rain in twenty-four hours marooning hundreds of people on the wrong side of the river from their camps. Flood stage continued several days. All kinds of craft were pressed into service for ferrying people but the best were Indians with dugout canoes. There were hundreds of other small incidents. The usual percentage of lost people, car wrecks on the congested road, disputes over who killed the game, camps placed too close to the river bank washed away when the river rose while the owners were out hunting, etc. One night we were awakened by a pounding on the station door. A somewhat drunk hunter said his partner had not returned to camp. Questioning him got little helpful information.*
>
> *Finally "grasping at straws" I asked how his partner was dressed. In reply the man said he had on a red hat. Since everybody in the area was wearing a red hat I took considerable ribbing from my partners for not being able to identify the man immediately from this useful (?) information. [sic]*

*First official party reaching top of Hurricane Ridge by auto over newly completed CCC Road from Elwha Camp, Chris Morgenroth second from right, November 1933. Courtesy Katherine Morgenroth Flaherty*

*CAMP ELWHA, PORT ANGELES, WASHINGTON F-17*

*Cat, Grader and Truck One Mile From Idaho Shelter, Elevation 5230 Feet, Hurricane Ridge, November 28, 1933. Road Construction With CCC Labor, Forest Service Equipment and Supervision, Chris Morgenroth, Foreman. Bailey Range in Background*

*Building Public Campgrounds Elwha Forest Camp, ca. 1936*

*CCC CAMP SNIDER, F-16. Photos by K. D. Swan, August 1933*

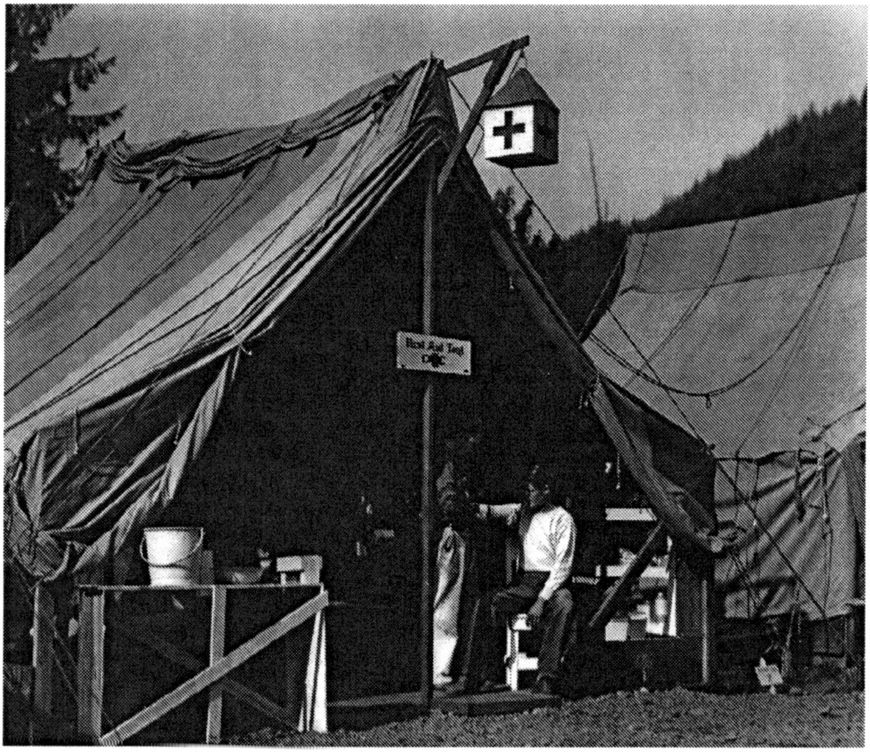

*Winter Sportsmen Meeting, Supervisor John R. Bruckart (center) Olympic National Park Superintendent Preston Macy (2nd row, right)*

*Jack Schwartz (left), Ed Cliff and others, Elk Study, ca. 1937*

*Elk Exclosure, Jack Schwartz, ca. 1937*

*University of Washington Students, Elk Study, ca. 1935–38*

*Left to Right: Leo Couch, Milo Perkins, Regional Forester C. J. Buck, Secretary of Agriculture Henry Wallace and Thornton T. Munger Hoh River, July 1935*

*Field Inspection, Ed Cliff (right) (Later Chief of the Forest Service) Jack Schwartz (left) Wildlife Biologist, ca. 1937*

*Preservation is retention undisturbed and in a natural condition, such as a museum. Conservation is the wise use of our environmental resources for the best interest of man. Of necessity, it involves a sense of stewardship and responsibility in the use of those resources. We undoubtedly need some preservation. But it cannot be the answer to the control of man's environment, for we are an ecological part of that environment, and to preserve it makes us a museum piece as well.*

*Melville Bell Grosvenor, Editor of "National Geographic" Magazine*

The executive order issued June 10, 1933, which transferred the Mt. Olympus National Monument to the National Park Service, was a significant event which was to have a lasting effect on the Olympic Peninsula. Change in administrative control of the monument to the National Park Service was to manifest itself in polarized views which have lasted for years. The controversy continues to this day in the small towns where stump ranchers and peninsula loggers gather with fishermen and mill workers over coffee or a stronger beverage.

The campaign to enact National Park status was waged by politicians and a committee of park advocates from "back east" led by Mrs. Rosalie Edge. These advocates were supported by local civic groups, some businessmen, and the Seattle Mountaineers Club. Harold Ickes, fiery Secretary of the Interior, was the driving force behind the movement for expansion of the National Park System and the creation of a Department of Conservation under one cabinet officer.

Forest Supervisor Bruckart recalls in his memoirs:

> *The Park Service sought and largely obtained public support from many preservation minded organizations and worked diligently to persuade the local people around the Peninsula (of) the economic advantages that would be gained by having a national park on the Olympic Peninsula. Also there was nation wide support sought and to a considerable degree obtained from many so called conservation groups. While there was considerable local support for the establishment of an Olympic National Park, particularly around Port Angeles and Forks, there was strong opposition in the Grays Harbor area.*

As a reaction to the Olympic Park Plan of the Emergency Conservation Committee of New York City, Regional Forester C. J. Buck was instructed by the Washington Office to present the controversy directly to civic groups and to involve the "grass root" communities. In a speech to the Aberdeen Chamber of Commerce on May 22, 1934, Buck emphasized the economic factors and impacts to the timber industry and local communities. Regional Forester Buck directed Ed Hanzlik of his staff to prepare an informal write-up summarizing the Forest Service position (dated

*Supervisor Plumb Studies the Upper Duckabush. Photo by F. W. Cleator, August 1927*

*Looking Southeast From Ridge East of Martins Park, Base of Mt. Christie to Right. Photo by F. W. Cleater, August 1927*

*Professor Edmond Meany, Historian, Mountaineer, Early Backer of the Press Expedition, and Johnny Bush, Seattle Mountaineers Olympic Expedition, 1920. Special Collections Division, University of Washington Libraries, negative no. UW12941*

*North Side of Mt. Anderson, 1918 Photo by R. L. Fromme*

*Mt. Anderson Valley of the Silt, 1920. Special Collections Division University of Washington Libraries, photo by R. L. Fromme, negative no. UW 7233*

August 26, 1936). The old Olympic veteran, Rudo Fromme, was detailed from the Mt. Baker National Forest to marshal support for the Forest Service. His public relations skills were quickly put to work. His recollection of this period in time helps to put the events in perspective:

> *About this time I received a call from Regional Forester C. J. Buck to come to Portland on a several weeks detail to help round up opposition to this proposed change to Park status. I was assigned to contacting labor unions, affiliated with the logging industry, in particular. Soon, armed with specially colored maps, statistics and my personal knowledge, I called on loggers unions in Portland, Tacoma, Grays Harbor and other Olympic Peninsula ports, obtaining interested audiences everywhere with this threat of loss of thousands of future jobs in timber harvesting, as well as public revenue to adjacent communities, now possible under the Multiple Use principle of National Forest Administration. My largest and most responsive audience was at a Union Loggers Convention at Raymond, on Willapa Harbor.*

With Fromme's return to the Olympic, he also prepared a report outlining the arguments against the establishment of a national park in the Olympics. With a concise, logical writing style, he enumerated sixteen pertinent points which effectively defended the multiple-use concept of land and resources so fundamental to Forest Service policy and objectives. His arguments focused on the subsidiary effects of "single-use" or only recreational values at the expense of mining, timber harvest, hunting and fishing considerations. The cost effectiveness of unwarranted duplication of manpower and authority was further offered as testimony for avoiding administrative changes.

By 1936, the concerns and rhetoric heightened controversy. Bob Marshall and his co-founders of the Wilderness Society were straddling both sides of the issue and were reluctant to endorse or lobby for national park status. No support for either agency position was made until May 1936 when wilderness values prevailed in favor of a national park.

A special committee on the Olympic National Park proposal convened in January 1935. Major O. A. Tomlinson, superintendent of Mt. Rainier National Park, wrote to the Washington State Planning Council and proposed this recommendation:

> *It is a well established policy that an area to receive the approval of the National Park Service for park status must measure up in every way to the high standard of scenic attractiveness, historic or scientific interest and appeal that characterize the national parks already established. Scenery must be of distinctive quality or there must be some natural feature so extra-ordinary or unique as to be of national interest and importance. In addition, areas considered for park status should be extensive and susceptible of such development along national park policies as may become necessary to permit the proper enjoyment of the area by the people.*
>
> *It is the unanimous opinion of all National Park Service officials who have inspected and studied the Mount Olympus area that the region in and adjacent to the Monument measures up fully to all national park standards and that it is worthy of the highest classification the Federal Government can bestow upon any land area, which is that of a national park.*
>
> *In view of the fact that this information is submitted to the State Planning Council before the Director of the National Park Service has acted upon the recommendations, it will be appreciated if the matter is treated as confidential pending further comment by the National Park Service. [sic]*

The committee received a memorandum prepared by subcommittee member, Leo Couch, who represented the Biological Survey of the U.S. Government. His viewpoint contradicted Major Tomlinson's position statements:

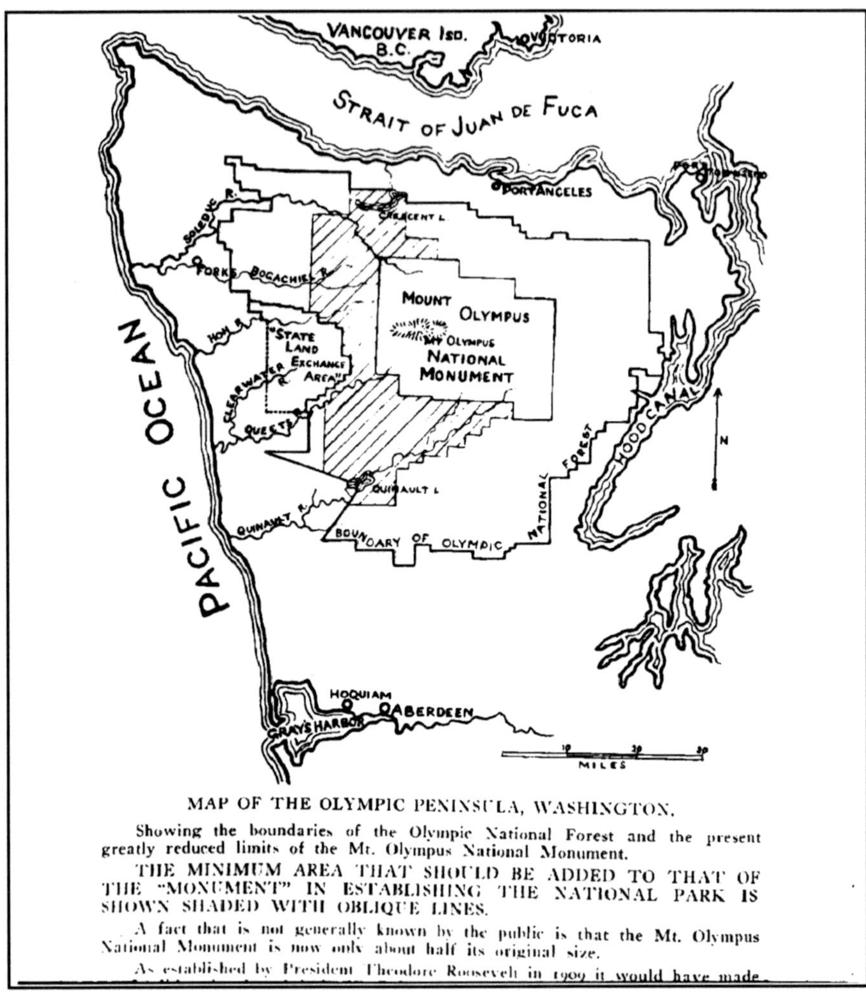


MAP OF THE OLYMPIC PENINSULA, WASHINGTON.

Showing the boundaries of the Olympic National Forest and the present greatly reduced limits of the Mt. Olympus National Monument.

THE MINIMUM AREA THAT SHOULD BE ADDED TO THAT OF THE "MONUMENT" IN ESTABLISHING THE NATIONAL PARK IS SHOWN SHADED WITH OBLIQUE LINES.

A fact that is not generally known by the public is that the Mt. Olympus National Monument is now only about half its original size.

As established by President Theodore Roosevelt in 1909 it would have made

*I understand the Special Committee on Mount Olympus National Monument will consider, this coming Saturday, the report of the National Park Service on their investigations of the proposed Mount Olympus National Park.*

*I have read the report and am familiar with its contents. While the recommendation is to make the area a wilderness national park, the pressure from the public to open up roads, auto camps, chalets, and hostels will be so great that the park could not remain a wilderness area very long. Already preliminary road routes are being suggested from the Quinault, through the Dosewalips and Elwha Rivers. The opening up and developing of this area would fill the heart of the Olympic with people in the summer months, when the elk are utilizing the summer range. This would, in a measure, defeat the major purpose of the reservation, which is to serve as an elk refuge.*

*I have given the matter considerable thought, and feel that the standards as set forth in a national monument are more what we desire in the Olympics. One has only to visit the national parks to see how they*

Locked up in the Olympic National Park are large surplus areas of what is primarily forest-growing land with little or no recreational value. The forest crop—the annual growth from this surplus land, cannot be harvested by reason of the National Park Service laws. If the surplus areas of productive land were to be transferred from the National Park Service to



*have been developed through road building, administrative structures, and concessions.*

*Although the majority of our people seem to favor this type of development, in order that they may observe the nation's beauty spots in ease and comfort, the Olympic area does not fit into the picture. It was set aside primarily as a game refuge, with the national forest surrounding it acting as a buffer area between the wilderness and commercial enterprise.*

*I favor turning the administration of the Monument back to the U.S. Forest Service, who have protected and maintained the wilderness character of the area since 1905. This Federal agency can administer the area without additional personnel, and it specializes in fire fighting and trail development. The Forest Service can administer the game and fur resources of the entire Federal holdings, with the exception of the Indian Reservations, under Regulation C-20-A. Under this there would be ample provision for the conservation of wild life in the entire Olympic area. If this comes up for a vote, please vote for me in the negative. [sic]*

*Leo K. Couch*

H. L. Plumb noted in the record that:

*The Forest Service is now devoting approximately one-third of the time to CCC men to recreation and we have four camps of 800 men on the Olympic Peninsula, building camps and putting in fireplaces from fire protection standpoint. The CCC are working and this has to go on. Recreation is well taken care of. [sic]*

*Jack Schwartz, Trail Riders of the Wilderness, 1937*

Earlier testimony revealed that Major Tomlinson, Assistant Superintendent Macy and the Park Committee had failed to respond directly to Forest Supervisor Plumb:

> *They have never come to me for any information in regard to the extension of the boundaries and I have offered to the officials pictures and information regarding the monument. They prefer to work alone.*

Area newspapers reveled in the public battle which was sharply divided into pro- and anti-park. District Rangers Floe, Blodgett, Mapes, and Fulton faithfully sent news clippings to the Supervisor's Office recording the latest developments. The special assignment of Rudo Fromme supported the Forest Service cause for a wilderness management option to counter the preservation enthusiasts. One prominent convert to Fromme's personal public relations campaign was Northwest photographer Asahel Curtis. In Mr. Fromme's words:

*Jim LeCron Assistant Secretary of Agriculture on Trail Riders of the Wilderness Trip, 1937*

> *This was not too pleasing to the majority of the interests who had financed his trip, I'm sure. However, as he made his report and arguments sink in, I'm quite sure that Grays Harbor people generally swung over to the status quo. Of course, they expected more trail development than we had heretofore provided and they hoped for more national*

*Low Divide Chalet, Trail Riders of the Wilderness, 1937*

> *publicity. Curtis took his enlarged views, also his slides, to Washington when the Park question was being debated there in congressional committees. He steadfastly advocated and worked for the Forest Service viewpoint, and was a quite regular attendant of the more local meetings, which aired the two sides later on. [sic]*

Fromme's illustrated talks on the Olympic Park debate were generally well received and produced some group resolutions supporting the Forest Service wilderness concept. One notable exception was described with typical Fromme flair for the dramatic:

> *I was flattered to note that one of my illustrated addresses on the Olympic National Forest got a U.S. representative in Washington. It was a letter from Congressman Mon Walgren stating that he had just noted an item in his home paper, from Everett, Washington, where I had spoken before the Chamber of Commerce in opposition to the establishment of a National Park in the Olympics. He wrote that I seemed to be "sticking my neck out," or words to that effect, in broadcasting such opposition to the President's already published opinion favoring such action, and his announced plans to visit that locality very shortly.*

Wildlife biologist, Jack Schwartz, was in the field working on the Olympic elk study when he was instructed to represent local Forest Service interests during an Olympic field trip by the Trail Riders of the Wilderness, a group sponsored by the American Forestry Society. He accompanied the field trip into the Olympic Mountains during the entire fourteen-day trip. Ignar Olson and Earnest Vorhees of Quinault were the packers-guides assisted by six wranglers, cooks and assistants. Fred Overly represented the National Park Service while Jim LeCron, Assistant Secretary of Agriculture, was the

*Chris Morgenroth on Field Trip With Park Proponents, Including the Influential Mrs. Rosalie Edge*

ranking Forest Service representative. Supervisor Bruckart, Assistant Regional Forester Horton, and Staff Officer Paul Logan, joined up with the trailride midway along the trip itinerary. The splendor of the August outing was recorded by Asahel Curtis whose photographs made more friends for the Forest Service. A group of national park proponents led by Preston Macy, custodian of the Mt. Olympus Monument, rendezvoused in the Elwha drainage with the Trail Riders to champion their cause. Included in this Olympic Riders group was the formidable Chris Morgenroth who had renounced his former employer in favor of a preservationist stance. Morgenroths' apparent "defection" from the Forest Service camp was seen as a betrayal of loyalties by staunch conservation leaders. Chris had been lecturing to women's clubs and others in favor of the park. One district ranger, Leroy Olander, suggested that a counterattack be made to negate Morgenroth's efforts. Morgenroth had resurfaced in federal forestry circles during CCC days as a foreman at Camp Elwha. Rollin Shaw related that Chris fascinated young CCC boys with tales of pioneer days and encounters with wolves, elk, and cougar which were perceived as a threat to the very existence of the settlers. Morgenroth's sincerity and integrity were never in question. He rationalized that the establishment of a national park was a greater benefit to the peninsula and would protect much of the old-growth forests. He advocated a switch to a pulpwood-based economy instead of the traditional sawmill oriented approach.

At the April 1936 hearings on the proposed "Walgren Bill," testimony was given before the House Public Lands Committee for nine days. The citizens of Port Angeles sent Morgenroth to testify in favor of the park; Asahel Curtis, Fromme's convert, was one of those testifying for the Forest Service. Three hundred pages of testimony were recorded from private organizations and individuals from both sides. Secretary of the Interior Ickes attacked the Forest Service for its biased reliance on the role of timber in the economy. Then National Park Service Director Arno Cammerer painted the Forest Service as "exploiters." Associate Forester Kneipp and H. L. Plumb, in the absence of Henry Wallace and Chief Forester Silcox, represented the agency's view for the Department of Agriculture. Secretary Ickes used strong words to summarize the position of park proponents:

> *I should like to make this point: sustained-yield logging, multiple use, or any of the smooth-sounding techniques of the Forest Service are no substitute for a National Park and will not save an area of National Park quality. Neither will they replace trees that are centuries old after they once have been cut down. [sic]*

Associate Forester Kneipp expressed the agency position and policy by denouncing the deluge of misinformation disseminated by public relations efforts of the "Eastern establishment" of park supporters.

> *This forest has been administered by the Forest Service since 1905, not without error, of course, because the whole thing was a grouping, as a part of a very radical readjustment of standard practices. But, as that Olympic Forest stands today, it is beautiful and it is protected and there are definite plans for its permanent protection and at the same time, it is an integration of economic activity and life and there has been until recently, only a single agency of administration which is most economic. Why should it be changed? [sic]*

Bob Marshall, one of the leading exponents of wilderness, had used his personal magnetism and wide social contacts to convey the argument that recreational values needed emphasis by the Forest Service.

The Wilderness Society carefully analyzed the contrasting agency advocacies and felt the best alternative was the establishment of Olympic National Park. With perhaps a twist of strange irony, Chief Forester Silcox hired Bob Marshall away from the Department of Interior in May of 1937 to fill a new position as Chief of Recreation and Lands.

The culmination of the national park controversy occurred in a theatrical and politically contrived fashion when it was announced that President Roosevelt would visit the Olympic Peninsula in person following the dedication of Timberline Lodge and an inspection of Grand Coulee Dam, (two of his proud "New Deal" projects). The President's announced visit involved elaborate preparations. Supervisor John Ray Bruckart tells about the preliminary plans in his memoirs:

*I was advised by the Regional Forester to report to the Regional Office in Portland to make plans for the President's trip which was to take place in about ten days. A party was organized headed by Regional Forester, C.J. Buck, his secretary Mildred Sinnott, Allan Hodgson, H. L. Plumb, and myself. The party drove around the Peninsula deciding various things to be accomplished before the Presidential party arrived. This among other things, (consisted) of assembling material with photographs explaining Forest Service management policies to be made available to news people traveling with the President. [sic]*

*The balance of the party returned to Portland while I stayed in Olympia to implement plans on the ground that had been decided upon by the Regional Forester and his staff. Later, Herb Plumb and I were directed to meet Col. Starling, Chief of the White House Secret Service Detail, in Port Angeles and accompany him over the route the President would travel. This included a brief inspection of the accommodations at Lake Crescent Inn on Lake Crescent, short stops at the Snider Ranger Station where the Ranger with the assistance of CCC enrollees were scheduled to put on a brief demonstration of forest fire prevention and Assistant Regional Forester, Ed Kavanaugh was to read a script prepared by Rudo Fromme explaining the action taking place. A stop was made at the Bloedell Logging Company where plans were made for a high climber to demonstrate topping a tall Douglas fir tree. A rest stop was planned at Kalaloch. Inspection was made of the Quinault Lodge where the party would have lunch. From Quinault, the route to be covered (went) through Hoquiam, Aberdeen, Montesano and on to Olympia. Col. Starling was pleased with the Forest Service (plan) for the trip. The trip with Starling ended in Olympia at 2 a.m. [sic]*

*Plans for (the) President's trip (were) completed October 1, 1937 and on the afternoon of October 2, the Presidential party arrived (at Port Angeles) on a U.S. destroyer from Victoria, B.C. at about 4 p.m. A fleet of Forest Service sedans with drivers, was assembled for members of the party with the addition of two large sedans for the President and (the) Secret Service Detail. [sic]*

Jack Schwartz was assigned as one of the drivers for the President's entourage of politicians, officials, and press. He recalls his shock at the President's arrival in Port Angeles, when the extent of Roosevelt's polio condition became apparent during the transfer from a naval vessel to a Forest Service vehicle. President Roosevelt reviewed the select cadre of forest officers at Singer's Tavern at Lake Crescent. Jack and Roger (Spike) Young were ordered back to Olympia as their vehicles were not needed for the rest of the loop journey.

*Waiting for the President, Port Angeles, Washington, October 2, 1937*

*President Roosevelt's Visit,*
*Snider Ranger Station,*
*October 3, 1937*

Mildred Neal (nee Sinnott) adds a poignant footnote to the preparations for the presidential visit:

> *During the trip it became apparent the President would need quarters other than that planned for him. The steps were too narrow for a wheel chair. New plans had to be made. Finally, the Regional Forester, C.J. Buck was asked to stay in the Inn and it was necessary for President Roosevelt to be quartered in one of the cabins with a ground floor entrance, surrounded by guards.*

*President Franklin D. Roosevelt and John R. Bruckart, October 3, 1937*

From Port Townsend to Tacoma, the response to the President's visit was enthusiastic by the local residents and press. The eastern contingent of twenty columnists and news correspondents accompanying the Chief Executive on his western tour also provided a glimpse to the nation of the isolated northwest corner once dubbed the last frontier. The *Port Angeles Evening News* was generous in praise of the logistical support and preparations handled by the Forest Service:

> *Like Robin Hood's men of old, these forest-green-clad officials and employees are everywhere today.*
>
> *The green-clad men of the U.S.F.S. waiting at the dock along with policemen from Seattle to drive cars for the presidential party, were a splendid-appearing group. They're a clean-cut type all the way through, and their stalwart figures in neat uniforms made a pleasing sight.*

*President Roosevelt at Lake Quinault Lodge, Princess Taholah and Princess Hoquiam (center) Melbourne Twins (left) Citizens of Taholah and Lake Quinault, October 3, 1937. Photo Seattle Post Intelligencer Collection, Museum of History and Industry, Seattle, Washington*

A memorandum dated six days after the presidential visit was written by Supervisor Bruckart:

*Olympia, Washington*
*Boundaries, Olympic*
*Mt. Olympus National Monument*
*October 6, 1937.*

*MEMORANDUM*

*On the evening of September 30, the Regional Forester, C. J. Buck, advised that the President wished me to come to his cottage for the purpose of pointing out the location of the large timber in the Forest on the area covered by the Wallgren bill. I spent something over half an hour in the cottage with the President, Regional Forester C. J. Buck, Senators Bone and Schwellenbach, Congressmen Smith and Wallgren, Major Tomlinson and Macey of the Park Service, and J. D. Ross, City Light Department, Seattle... [sic]*

Bruckart explained the different forest types, cutting practices, and general topic of forest and use management. Roosevelt asked some penetrating questions regarding elk and selective logging, and Bruckart capably responded with the Forest Service position.

The rustic Singers Lodge was the temporary Western White House. Rudo Fromme, the artful man for all occasions related the following about the historic visit to the Olympic National Forest:

*I was also requested to attend the conference-banquet at Singer's Resort and the F.S. fire equipment demonstration at the Snider Ranger Station at the time of the President's visit to Lake Crescent, north and west sections of the Olympic Forest and Peninsula. Incidentally, I had the pleasure of giving up my warm hotel room at Singer's Resort on the day of the banquet conference to the John Boettiger family, while the four of them were assembled in my room to speed the takeover, they had found the cabin assigned too chilly. I drove to the above mentioned ranger station for lodging after the banquet conference between Regional Forester Buck and President Franklin D. Roosevelt.*

*After the president and his retinue were properly parked for viewing the fire equipment demonstration mid-morning the next day, the fire pump refused to cooperate, even though tested satisfactorily just prior to the arrival of the august audience. The consequent delay and background activity caused Ranger Floe's saddle and pack horse to become so excited that he had to get out of view at once. Regional Forester Buck, who had been sitting with the president in the front seat of the head car, slipped around to me, saying that the president wasn't paying any attention to Kavanaugh's well prepared loud speaker speech, hidden from view, and requesting that I get the president's ear, if possible, to explain the intended demonstration, apologize and offer to supply any information he might request.*

*Well, I got the president's ear for perhaps a minute. He smiled and nodded automatically, then interrupted with, "How's the road to that hotel where we are to have lunch? Do they serve pretty good eats?" A couple of hours later, when I reached the Quinault Lake hotel, Mrs. McNeill, the hostess and chief cook, was beaming beautifully. She burst forth with, "Oh! the President was thrilled with our cooking. My! Did he eat! He took seconds on almost everything."*

In a letter to Forest Supervisor Bruckart, Ed Kavanaugh, Assistant Regional Forester, cited the cooperation of the following Forest Service men during President Roosevelt's visit:

*1. Dispatcher: Bert Johnson*

*1a. Ranger: Mr. Floe*
*Horse holder: Al Reese*
*Radioman: Bill Tonkin*

*2. Smoke Chasers:*
*Morris, Olson*

*3. Fire Squad (Al Reese, Gong Man), Osborne, Alexander, Wright*

*Johnson, Simoni, Lasham, Radich, Macauley, Forsythe*

*4. Packer and String:*
*Packer - Oscar Peterson*

*5. Truck Trailer Unit:*
*K. Simons - Drivers*
*(Art Tennol sitting on Cat)*

*6. Faller's Outfits:*
*Alexander, Wright*

*7. Hose Pump Man:*
*Allen - Johnson*

*8. Pump in Operation:*
*Larsen - Pump man*
*Wolfe - Nozzleman*
*Rey - Helper*

*9. Fire Truck:*
*(Cecil Rud Driving)*
*Fire Squad*

With the establishment of the Olympic National Park, the gradual phasing out of Forest Service buildings, roads, trails began. Many structures were simply utilized by the park in lieu of constructing new facilities. Mr. E. B. Webster had donated the Heart of the Hills Klahane Gardens to the Olympic National Forest in perpetuity in October 1936. Wildlife expert Jack Schwartz was selected to oversee the renamed E. B. Webster Memorial Garden because he had some background in botany; a professional botanist assisted in the cataloguing of exotic plants. As a result of administrative changes in 1938, the gardens were considered incompatible with park management policy and they were abandoned.

*E.B. Webster Gardens Memorial Sign*

The custodial era ended for the Forest Service with the advent of World War II. Ranger Bill Bryan summed up the transition to a management system of the forest rather than merely acting as caretaker for the publicly owned forest. Excerpts from Bryan's letter to Regional

Forester J. Herbert Stone provide insights:

> *In 1937 selective cutting in Douglas-fir was gaining importance, mainly because the higher value Douglas-fir could be removed while leaving the low value hemlock. Axel Brandstrom of the Experiment Station and Newell of the Regional office persuaded Schafers to try selective cutting on their West Fork Satsop sale. The first logs were removed in November, 1937. Tree selection cutting continued until 1941 when log values increased, permitting removal of hemlock. Thereafter it was clear cutting by staggered units with high-lead and skidder... [sic]*
>
> *The present Satsop Guard Station was sale headquarters. The dwellings and office was built during 1939-41 by CCC personnel. I lived there from 1937 to 1945. Other TSO's assigned to this sale included Newell Cory, Vern Hicks, J. O. F. Anderson, Estel Brown, Earl Simonton, Merle Moore, Howard Johnson, Pat Wick, Leslie Sullivan, John Carlson, and Ward Hall...*
>
> *In 1944 the Hoodsport district was de-activated and the Shelton district formed which included the South Fork Skokomish and Wynoochee drainages. The balance of the Hoodsport district went to Quilcene. I moved to Shelton in the Spring of 1945 as district ranger... [sic]*

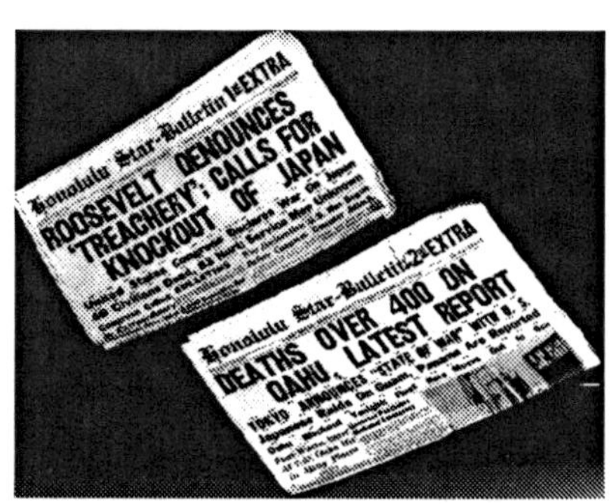

Honolulu Star-Bulletin 1st EXTRA

ROOSEVELT DENOUNCES 'TREACHERY'; CALLS FOR KNOCKOUT OF JAPAN

Honolulu Star-Bulletin 2nd EXTRA

DEATHS OVER 400 ON OAHU, LATEST REPORT

EXTRA The Aberdeen Daily World EXTRA

JAPAN OPENS WAR ON U.S.

Harbor Defense Units Stand By

Planes Bomb Honolulu, Pearl Harbor, 250 Killed

BOMBS RAIN ON ISLAND CAPITAL CITIZENS WATCH

U.S. Cabinet Leaders To Meet Tonight

NAVAL MEN OF COAST PLACED ON WAR FOOTING

> *At that time Dahl Kirkpatrick was preparing the management plan and agreement for the proposed Shelton Coop. Sustained Yield Unit, and made several trips to Shelton. In 1946 the agreement with Simpson was consummated, effective January 1, 1947. [sic]*
>
> *The coop. unit brought on changes from the normal procedure, especially in the field of long range planning and recorded keeping. Unfortunately, Simpson's operations in the Skokomish were abandoned in 1946 and centered in the Wynoochee. The change over from railroad to truck roads also occurred about this time. Truck road construction and logging started together. The need to meet the raw material demand of the mills resulted in some poor road planning and overcutting in the Wynoochee until 1950, when operations started on Canyon River and were resumed in the Skokomish. [sic]*

Eyes Aloft

A PUBLICATION FOR MEMBERS OF THE AIRCRAFT WARNING SERVICE

VOL. 2 — No. 9 DECEMBER, 1943

# AWS ALERT STATUS PROVES BIG SUCCESS

**AAF Chief Thanks AWS Members For Vital Work**

**System Operates Within Few Minutes During Test Trials**

*I looked for planes till my eyes were ready to drop out...*

*Winona Harner*

Supervisor Neal was the last of "Pinchot's Boys" to serve on the Olympic. He was to guide the forest through the difficult war years which had drained the fire protective forces for military service. Wood was essential for the war effort as it had many practical uses; further demands were imposed upon the Pacific Northwest by the threat of Japanese invasion. Drastic measures were called for and the Olympic responded. Lloyd E. Brown vividly described his role during those critical times in the July 1977 edition of the *Timberlines* Region Six, 30 Years Club publication:

*During World War II the Forest Service had supervision of the Aircraft Warning Service for the Army. This job was assigned to the Division of Engineering, under James Frankland, Regional Engineer. I was transferred, in the fall of 1942, to Engineering, to fill one of the two supervisory jobs in the AWS unit to fill a vacancy. The region had supervision of all of the AWS lookout posts in Oregon and Washington, where it was necessary to have paid observers. This included points on the National Forests, National Parks, Indian Reservations, and State and Private lands, under State Forester's Supervision. In cities and towns the observation posts were manned by volunteers, under the Civil Defense Agency. The AWS posts had to be manned by two people to provide 24-hour, daily observation. They had to have telephone or radio communication to their army filter centers and to their supervisory headquarters. Generally, all of these observation posts in Region Six, covered the areas quite thoroughly, from the Pacific Ocean to the Cascade Mountains, and From California to the Canadian border, and along the Canadian border to Idaho. Keeping the AWS posts supplied with food and fuel as well as keeping communications working in the winter with deep snow was difficult at times.*

**FLASH MESSAGE FORM**

Call your telephone central and say: "ARMY FLASH ______________ "
(Give your phone number)
Central will connect you with an Army Information Center.
When you hear: "ARMY, GO AHEAD PLEASE", you say: "FLASH"
and continue message you have checked on form below, in the order indicated:

| 1 | 2 | 3 | 4 | 5 | 6 | 7 | 8 |
|---|---|---|---|---|---|---|---|
| NUMBER OF AIRPLANES | TYPE OF AIRPLANES | ALTITUDE OF AIRPLANES | WERE AIRPLANES SEEN OR HEARD? | YOUR OBSERVATION POST CODE NAME | DIRECTION OF AIRPLANES FROM O. P. | DISTANCE OF AIRPLANES FROM O. P. | AIRPLANES HEADED TOWARD |
| (Number) | SINGLE-MOTOR | VERY LOW | | | NW N NE | (Miles) | NW N NE |
| | BIMOTOR | LOW | SEEN | | W E | | W E |
| FEW | MULTI-MOTOR | HIGH | HEARD | | SW S SE | | SW S SE |
| MANY | | VERY HIGH | | | If airplanes were directly over O. P. cover columns 6 and 7 by reporting: "OVERHEAD" | | Omit if it will cause delay in report. |

*Bill Parke had supervision of the Oregon AWS posts and I had the Washington area, and we worked with the Supervisors of the various agencies. The purpose of the Aircraft Warning Service was to prevent Japanese planes from attacking the U.S. The observers had to report every plane they saw or heard to their filter center immediately. Private planes were banned from the area, so the only planes to report were military or commercial passenger planes. If an observer failed to report a plane that should have been within 6 miles of his post, the Army called it a miss. Two misses, and we had to go to the post, sometimes on snowshoes, to see what caused the miss, such as observers absent, communication failed, or could not see or hear the plane because of storms. [sic]*

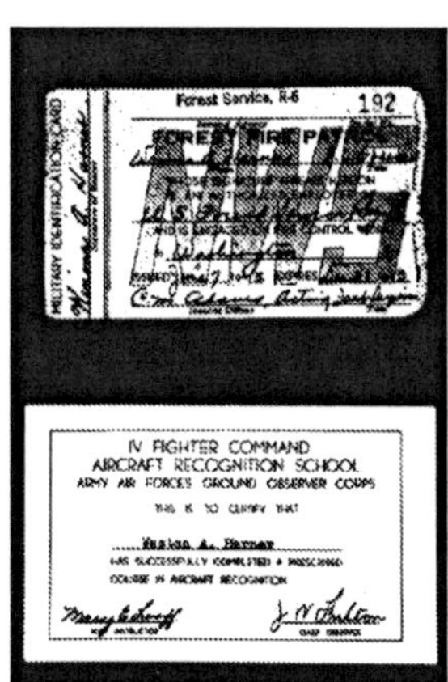


Under the direction of the U.S. Army, the Aircraft Warning Service or AWS was formed in 1942 when the country was in imminent danger of attack from Japanese forces. The Forest Service was the coordinating agency for the establishment of AWS observation posts; existing fire lookouts were used and makeshift cabins and structures were constructed to augment the Forest Service lookout system. The U.S. Coast Guard also participated in the program. Forest Service lookouts within the boundaries of the newly-created Olympic National Park were also manned, with Dodger Point and Blue Mountain lookouts as prime examples. In addition, the Enchanted Valley Chalet was occupied as an observer post. Quinault pioneer, Ignar Olson, packed supplies to the chalet during the AWS occupancy (1942-1944). Weston A. Harner and his wife, Winona, from Montesano, were recruited as relief observers at eight aircraft warning stations within the

*Volunteer Armband for AWS Observer*

jurisdiction of the Quinault Ranger District whose local official was Ranger Joe Fulton. The eight designated observation posts were: Baker L.O., Sea-Lion L.O., O'Took L.O., Matheny L.O., Higley Peak L.O., Neilton L.O., Humptulips L.O., and Burnt Hill L.O. The district ranger station maintained three dispatchers who worked 8-hour shifts so that communication lines were open on a 24-hour basis.

*Winona Harner at Baker Lookout Just Inland a Few Miles From Point Grenville, a Coast Guard Station*

During her stint of duty, Winona Harner kept a daily diary, and selected excerpts follow:

> *October 8, 1942 - Left Quinault at 8:30 started hiking at 10 to 9. Arrived at Higley Peak at about 12:00. Relieved Thor Thorson and Frank Smith. Jumped an elk on the climb up. What a climb too. Started raining at about 3:15 visibility nil.* [sic]

> *October 9, 1942 - Wes took watch at 4:a.m. I woke up; cooked breakfast about 9:a.m. Wes talked with J. Fulton at 8:45. Rained all night. Frog in the dishpan of rain water this a.m. Chipmunks very tame. Caught water in pans for washing etc. Have to go skimpy on the water. The view is wonderful from here. You can see all over the Olympics nearly.* [sic]

> *December 24, 1942 - O'Took [observation post]*

> *December 25, 1942 - It snowed during night. About 1 1/2... You should see my Christmas tree. Its a hemlock branch and a few branches of salal with bits of our pkg. wrapping strings tied on for decorations. Looks like a little tree anyway. Quite festive.* [sic]

> *January 29, 1943 - Sea Lion ...State of activity today. Beautiful day - sunshine. Wes took a hike down the new road. We cut wood about 5:p.m. We had a plane flash then 2-P-38's. There are boats off shore also tonight and all night...* [sic]

> *March 3, 1943 - Mr. Fulton, came and installed different phone line at Burnt Hill. He said he hoped we would stay on as relief operators cause it was hard to get anyone for the job. Gee it was a pretty day. I looked for planes till my eyes were ready to drop out...* [sic]

> *April 15, 1943 - Had our first Flying Fortress today - was it beautiful in the sky. Mr. Fulton, stopped. I was picking lillies across the canyon and I sent some to the office. Wes had the car all apart today; found a dead mouse under the seat. We had elk steak...*[sic]

> *April 24, 1943 - ...Wes was listening to the short wave last night at 12:15. He finished up Tokyo. The announcer said that the (Japs) were beating the U.S. and that the Philipinos were very happy under their new leaders...*[sic]

*April 29, 1943 - Higley Peak - We left about 9:00, arrived at the Peak in 2hrs & 5 min. 8 soldier divisions of the mechanized cavalry from Quinault Army Base helped pack our supplies up. Mr. Fulton, Mr. Frist also went up. We were in better shape this trip than last.*

*May 10, 1943 - Went to Sea Lion... Wes sent in flash on blinking light seen at 9:45.*

*May 11, 1943 - Army came to investigate light at 2:15 in the a.m. I was just up and Wes had just got to sleep and did they scare me...*

*Winona Harner at Sea Lion Lookout. Courtesy Winona Hammonds (nee Harner)*

*Wes Harner on Trail to Higley Peak.*
*Courtesy Winona Hammonds (nee Harner)*

*Howard "Bo" Elder, Protective Assistant and Mrs. Vera First, Radio Operator and Dispatcher*
*Courtesy Winona Hammonds (nee Harner)*

"On Duty" Quinault District Ranger Joe Fulton World War II Era

*May 15, 1943 - (We had 6 plane flashes by 3:30 - Can't get return from 98 so don't know if they were received or not. The radio is so damn noisy you can hear only static. This plane is searching for the last flyer and Wes saw running lights once. The flashes didn't get through and I turned them all in at 8:20 - Be a fine thing if it was Japs landing they could take over and we would be S.O.L.)...* [sic]

*May 17, 1943 - Burnt Hill ...Mr. Fulton, Bo Elder and Ed Hanzlik (from Olympia) were here - brought their lunch and I made them coffee... Wes spied a Navy blimp today off the coast and looked like a disabled aircraft carrier traveling by two ocean going vessels...*

*August 19, 1943 - (Abels Slash Fire: At nine 35 or 40 this morning the fog lifted and I spotted this fire. I watched it for a few minutes, then reported it to the Ranger Station. 9:45. About 10:15, Bo Elder came up and called Mr. Fulton, and told him just about where he thought it was and then left to go to the fire)...*

*December 28, 1943 - The F.S.-AWS - Radio Tech., installed a high frequency radio here at Burnt Hill today. He fixed our radio, too. Works much better. Mr. Fulton and Cal helped. They came about 9 o'clock and the Tech. Mr. Kresik, didnt' leave till 4::30 about. We had a Drill Alert from 10:40 a. to 5:p.).* [sic]

*Christmas Day, December 25, 1943.*

*May 31, 1944 - ...Raining again for this last day of A.W.S. Mildred is glad it is ending but I'm not. Wes will go to fire guard school and then be fire lookout this summer here at Burnt Hill.* [sic]

Eva Cook Taylor, Log Scaler During World War II, Quilcene District, 1943

In 1941, Eva Cook Taylor attended the Olympic National Forest Fire Guard Training School which was held at Hoodsport. Eva wasn't bothered by the fact that she was the only female on the roster of trainees. Long-time check-scaler J. Denny Ahl and his wife took her under their wing and she stayed with them during Fire Guard School. Eva became AWS lookout on Mt. Townsend and recalls her remote post as one of the best times in her life. Daughter of a logger, she loved the woods and gloried in the freedom of the back country. Jack "Whiskers" Conrad, who worked a number of seasons for the Quilcene Ranger District, taught her to "throw a diamond hitch" and

*Burnt Hill. Courtesy Winona Hammonds (nee Harner)*

*Jack "Whiskers" Conrad and friend, Quilcene District, 1941*

*Wes Harner at Higley Peak. Courtesy Winona Hammonds (nee Harner)*

*AWS Station Believed to be O'Took Lookout. Courtesy Winona Hammonds (nee Harner)*

**F I N A L   S O U V E N I R   E D I T I O N**

# Eyes Aloft

A PUBLICATION FOR MEMBERS OF THE AIRCRAFT WARNING SERVICE

VOL. 2 — No. 12 MAY, 1944

## CIVILIAN AWS TO BE INACTIVATED

PAGE TWO *A Publication for Members of the Aircraft Warning Service* EYES ALOFT

Alert-eyed Harold Conklin, AWS observer, did well the day he spotted a Jap sub shelling the oil fields of Elwood, California. Conklin's call brought planes.

## AWS in Review

With the thought, "Always On the Alert," still in the minds and hearts of 150,000 Pacific Coast civilian volunteers, the Aircraft Warning Service this month went into military retirement.

The order inactivating the AWS closed a very colorful and important chapter in the history of United States participation in World War II.

In 1941 and 1942, long before the days of thousand plane American air attacks, and U. S. naval superiority, the citizens of the Pacific Coast waited determinedly for enemy air attacks. Had we been attacked, the enemy would have discovered an efficient, well-knit air warning service ready and waiting to send fighter planes into the air to meet the attack, — an organization composed of plain American citizens who had responded to their nation's appeal for help.

In those early and disheartening days, the civilian volunteers who gave so freely of their time and energies could well feel proud of their organization, for they knew it was their job to stand between the enemy and our vital war industries and our homes. They were there as a branch of the Army Air Forces, and they did their job as thor-

EXTRA The Aberdeen Daily World

JAPAN SURRENDERS

B-29s Loose 6,000 Tons Of Destruction

Reds Shatter Jap Defenses In Manchuria

Defeated Enemy Accepts Unconditional Demand Hirohito Will Aid Allies

President Announces Victory At End Of Long Day Of Waiting; M'Arthur To Head Occupation

149 Twin City Heroes Give Lives In War

Federal Manpower Sirens Herald

how to pack a horse or mule. Eva mastered packing by practicing with wooden match boxes on a kitchen table. The old bachelor, Conrad, was a loner but a good teacher and "a bit of a boozer." Mt. Townsend, seventeen miles by trail was serviced by "Teddie," one of two mules who were stabled at a lean-to near the lookout. Eva had learned shorthand and was asked to do office work, but her greatest contribution to the Forest Service during WWII was as a log-scaler. She worked alongside Earl Simonton and received a superior rating from the regional check- scaler from Portland. Eva recalls John Bernston packing for the Quilcene District with about 15 or 20 head of stock quartered at the barn. Eva retained her love of the Olympics with frequent trail rides and has documented the early history of the Quilcene area, especially the efforts of the miners pursuing their dreams in *The Lure of Tubal-Cain*.

Early explorers hoped for untold wealth and riches to be found in the Olympic mountains, and later prospectors were undaunted by repeated failures of marginal claim operations within the boundaries of the Olympic Reserve. The miners were steadfast in their efforts and benefited from the liberal timber use permitted in mining activities. The establishment of the Mt. Olympus Monument within the Forest Reserve did curtail mining under the Antiquities Act of 1916. The prospectus of the Black and White Mine reflects on early mining efforts and the involvement of the Forest Service.

> *The Black and White Mine is located in the Sawtooth Range of the Olympic Mountains in the northwestern part of Mason County, Washington, and lies about one mile southeast of Mount Gladys and about two miles from the north branch of the Skokomish River. It is twenty-three miles by trail to the nearest deep water harbor at Potlatch, in Mason County, Washington, and is one hundred and ten miles by water from Potlatch to the Tacoma Smelting Co. located at Tacoma, Washington. [sic]*

*Tubal Cain Mine, September 1931*

*The elevation of the mine is 4000 feet, with a grade of not to exceed two per cent at any point of the road or proposed road, with the exception of the last one and one-half miles where the grade would be about four per cent. A very good County road has been built from Potlatch for a distance of ten miles to Lake Cushman, and the County and the United States Department of Forestry are about to build an additional five miles within the next year to a point in the Olympic Mountains known as the "Stair Case." From this point for a distance of three miles the United States Department of Forestry will join with the owners of the mine in building a roadway on a fifty-fifty basis, and from the end of this three-mile road will be two miles of roadway to be built to a point where the ore can be brought down by tramway a distance of two thousand feet to a loading bunker, which would avoid the four percent grade at the end of the road near the mine. At the present time there is a good trail all the way from Lake Cushman to the mine and building of the roadway will be along this trail with very few exceptions. [sic]*

Another early mining effort along the North Fork of the Skokomish was documented by Robert Keatts:

*In 1912, the Olympian Copper Company (presumably made up of several individuals with mining interests at the Black and White Mine) requested permission from the Forest Service to use downed timber in the area for constructing a six-to-eight-mile flume to transport ore from the mine. Although the Forest Service was agreeable to the plan, the flume was apparently never built (USFS ONF 1912, 22 July, 23, July, 6 August). Reportedly, in 1915, five tons of ore somehow were shipped to the Tacoma smelter where quantities of copper, iron, and silver were extracted. Around 1918, when the presence of copper was first recognized (Green 1945, 40), 100 tons of ore were shipped to the Bilrowe Alloys*

*Map of Coastal Washington Showing the Locations of Logging Dams*

Near West Fork Splash Dam, Chester Wilson With Maul on Shoulder

*Company in Tacoma. Lack of a feasible, economical means of transportation, however, continued to present difficulties for the claimholders. Possibly for that reason, the Black and White Mine was put up for sale in 1919.*

Mr. Keatts related that Smith Keller, George Thomas, and Joseph Moss, who were associated with the Smith Mine were a local novelty because they were black:

> *The curiosity grew to respect, and the Negroes were well liked by almost everyone. Several accounts verify the presence of Smith in the North Fork Skokomish River valley as early as 1890. In July of that year Lt. O'Neil's expedition recorded that Smith was operating in the mountains adjacent and in September, Smith was on a scow from Union City to Hoodsport. Other documentation reports that two Negroes were working at a coal mine located on the Purdy cut-off road north of Shelton. These men later drifted into the Olympics to look for their rainbow with its pot of gold at the end. Because of the year of this account (1897), I believe this may have been where two of the Negroes worked in the winter months. On the other hand, it may have been two who later joined Keller, Moss and Thomas...*
>
> *Each spring, about the middle of May, the Negroes arrive in Hoodsport where they secured their mules, purchased supplies and headed for their claim 25 miles into the Olympics. After the summer spent in the mountains, the men would come out about mid-October and return to their homes in Seattle for the winter. Their animals were wintered across Hood Canal from Potlatch at Dry Creek, and on occasion one Negro would stay with them. He would work at odd jobs to pay for his keep and look after the stock...*
>
> *...These men devoted their lives to a cause and in most respects made an honest living. The Forest Service compensated them with food because they usually opened up the trail in the spring, and as long as it didn't become a habit afforded them shelter when needed as they travelled to and from Hoodsport. [sic]*

The creation of the Olympic National Park in 1938 prohibited mining activities which had previously been acceptable under the jurisdiction of the Forest Service. The involvement of the Olympic National Forest in the demands imposed by World War II was not confined to manpower and timber. Manganese was an important component in the process of making steel, and vital in the manufacture of implements of war. A mine-to- market road functioned in the Quinault District; other prominent manganese mines were the Joseph Campbell operations located on the West Fork of the Humptulips River. The Forest Service Shelter and Campground commemorate this early miner. The most prolific manganese wartime mine was the Crescent Mine which was leased by the Sunshine Mining Company of Kellogg, Idaho. A prospectus at the time indicated the following:

> *The ore was mined through a tramming tunnel at railroad level and shipped here by Port Angeles Western Railroad. That ore was gold to the government, stockpiled on the port dock and after the war shipped to northern California...*
>
> *All operations of the Crescent mine were on a lease and royalty basis. The owners were Mrs. Chris Morgenroth, Port Angeles: T.F. Rixon, former resident; Chris Anderson, Dungeness; and the heirs of the late Joseph Marsh.*

A Morgenroth daughter, Katherine Flaherty, recently related:

> *Manganese from that mine put me and my sister through college...and that was during the Depression.*

The Forest Service has long recognized the importance of mineral resources and how exploration and development often serve the national interest.

The first commercial timber sale on the Olympic National Forest was on the West Fork of the Humptulips River in 1906. The sale was made to the Humptulips Driving Company which operated a series of splash dams on both branches of the river. Another early timber sale was located on the Duckabush River. This sale comprised a strip a mile long and a quarter mile wide, crossing the river at right angles. Cutting began in 1907 and the last timber was removed in August 1910.

The Humptulips River sales were typical in that they utilized the splash dam method of transportation first advocated by Theodore Rixon in his 1902 report. Ed Van Syckle describes the use of these early dams in *They Tried to Cut It All : A History of Logging in Grays Harbor County:*

> *Coincident with the skidroad was the splash (or sluice) dam, a method of releasing a large head of water into a stream bed to wash out collections of logs. It was first used by bullteam loggers, and later was highly instrumental in making the fore-and-aft skidroad a success. Logs pulled down from the hills were dumped into the rivers and in many cases splash- dam ponds.*

*West Fork Splash Dam #3, Humptulips River*

*Skid Road and Dam West Fork Humptulips*

*Waiting for a Splash on the Duckabush*

*"Splashing" West Fork Humptulips*

*Humptulips Driving Company*
*All Humptulips Photos Courtesy of Raleigh Wilson*

*West Fork Dam,*
*Humptulips Driving Company*

*Roll Dam, West Fork Humptulips*

*Polson Logging Co. Camp 1 Spur. Courtesy Polson Museum*

*Donkey Engine and Yarding Crew, Polson Logging Co. Courtesy Polson Museum*

*Simpson Logging Co. Headquarters Camp, ca. 1895. Courtesy David James, Simpson Timber Company*

*Logging With Ox Teams. Courtesy Polson Museum*

*"Iron Horses" Railraod Camp, Polson Logging Co. Courtesy Polson Museum*

*Ranger Bill Bryan, Dorothy Godwin (Washington Office), Supervisor Carl Neal, at Shafer Logging Co. Camp*

*Tools and Fallers Camp 2, Polson Logging Co., 1913. Courtesy Polson Museum*

*Camp 3 Cookhouse, Polson Logging Co. Courtesy Polson Museum*

*Ashley Poust Scaling Logs at the Reload*

*Skid Road, Polson Logging Co. Courtesy Polson Museum*

Polson Logging Co. "Gandy Dancers" Laying Track. Courtesy Polson Museum

*When water in the splash dams was released, the logs were carried in a torrent to tidewater - that is, those that did not hang up on gravel bars - and then it was the job of a crew and a small donkey engine, or sometimes other means, to "sack" the river, moving the stranded logs into the water... [sic]*

Tree Topping. Courtesy Polson Museum

*Then it was up to the booms at tidewater to catch the logs, sort them according to brands and ownership, and raft them for towing to the mill. It was also the time the irate rancher went out to this riverbank to see how much land he had lost in the splash...*

*A number of streams had both splash and roll dams, the latter used largely for collecting logs and keeping them afloat. The roll dam was simplicity itself. It was built of cribbed logs, but had no sluice gates. Instead, it had well-secured brow logs (atop the dam) and a sloping apron into the stream below. As the water in the dam rose by freshet or water release upstream, the logs rolled over the brow pieces and on their way to tidewater.*

Railroad logging soon replaced the colorful splash dams and reached into the timbered valleys far beyond the location of the tidewater mills. Each of the big logging companies on the Peninsula had established camps in the woods, with crews coming and going. Soon the camps were portable, consisting of railcar bunkhouses frequently changing location when the timber supply was depleted. The methods of logging changed due to technology and so did the logger, according to Ed Van Syckle:

*Vance Creek Bridge, Built in 1929 by Simpson Timber Company. Courtesy Simpson Timber Company*

> *The logger himself had changed from a hell-roaring, kisser-punching, hard- drinking, harlot-hugging ramstam into a sober, hard-working fellow and family man, who left his spiked shoes in the bunkhouse and went home for weekends.*

*Big Load—Log Cut On Road To Camp Grisdale. Left to right: George L. Drake, Logging Superintendent Simpson Timber Company; Dave Adams; Bull Buck; Ed Elliot, Railroad Superintendent 1930s. Courtesy Simpson Timber Company*

The Olympic National Forest operated in a custodial oriented management mode during the Depression years of the 1930s and into the beginning of the next decade. The winds of change quickly fanned the winds of war which placed many demands on the Olympic forest. The development of plywood and veneer plants coupled with the rise of the pulp industry resulted in the utilization of the hemlock tree which previously had been considered an inferior waste wood. Many private timber companies had depleted their holdings and were eager to purchase the federal timber available on the Olympic National Forest.

The pioneer loggers, the Schafer Brothers, and the Polson Brothers, were major purchasers of federal timber sales both on the Olympic National Forest and the Quinault Indian Reservation. The wartime demands for fir and spruce intensified to the extent that even the Quinault Natural Area, and previously inviolate Olympic National Park, were candidates for supplying the raw materials. The Quinault Natural

*"Evolution of Donkey Engine." Dragging Out Logs With Geared Locomotive (left), and Ordinary Road Locomotive (right). Douglas Spruce District, Mason County*

Area was spared and left intact as forest resources in Alaska, the Skagit Valley, and Queets corridor were selected to supply the war effort. Olympic National Forest timber sales to Schafer Brothers in 1943 amounted to 852 million board feet of timber valued at almost four million dollars.

The dynasty started by prominent timberman Sol Simpson was interrupted unexpectedly with the death of his grandson, Sol Reed. The person selected to carry on the company tradition was George Lincoln Drake who was a graduate of Pennsylvania State College in Forestry with the class of 1912. His first job was cruising timber for the Forest Service in Oregon. During World War I, he was transferred to Alaska where he became Assistant Forest Supervisor at the time of Olympic Supervisor Fromme's detail in Alaska. During Drake's 19 year career with the Forest Service, he was instrumental in pioneering fire prevention programs and was recognized for his organizational and leadership abilities.

In a letter to Regional Forester, J. Herbert Stone, Snider Ranger Sanford Floe paid tribute to George Drake:

> *Supervisor Allen had recommended to Supervisor Plumb of the Deschutes that I be appointed to a Ranger vacancy on that Forest...I was slated for the Crescent District in the spring. Bert Nason was in charge of a sale to Brooks-Scanlon and I was assigned to him for a few weeks scaling and marking until another job came up as compass man for George Drake on a land exchange cruise.*
>
> *George arrived in a Ford Model "T" bearing U.S.F.S. license plate No. 1. This contraption was a World War I ambulance and we loaded our camping gear and grub on the platform in*

*back. The cruising George was to do involved two Forests, the Fremont and Deschutes. We finished the job in December. George was a wonderful teacher and I often wonder how I would have managed as a District Ranger later on if it had not been for his training in surveying and cruising on this job.*

George Drake's managerial skills were well utilized by Simpson as he was able to apply his Forest Service experience to logging, forestry, fire prevention, and community relations programs. Drake departed from the traditional logging camp approach by envisioning Camp Grisdale as a planned rural community that was people-oriented until its demise four decades later.

Dave James writes in *Grisdale, Last of the Logging Camps*:

*Grisdale would not have been built if Simpson had not won approval to enter a Sustained Yield contract with the U.S. Forest Service. In the years when Kreienbaum, with the backing of chairman W.G. Reed, negotiated terms for a 100-year cooperative contract into which Simpson put its lands, trees, and mills in Shelton and McCleary, the company was nearly out of Old Growth timber. In 1946, Simpson had about enough wood to supply its mills for eight more years. After that, it would have shut down McCleary and continued but one sawmill in Shelton. Thus the SYU contract extended employment life for the communities while millions of young trees on Simpson lands grew big enough to be cut now and in the future.*

*Neighboring Grays Harbor towns also won a federal Sustained Yield Unit, differing in that local companies put no lands or timber under common management with the Forest Service.*

In December 1944, the Portland meeting of the proceedings of the Western Forestry and Conservation Association was called to order by its President George L. Drake of Simpson who gave a talk entitled "Practical Forestry Comes of Age." Richard E. McCardle, later to become Chief of the Forest Service, addressed the group with the topic:

*THE COOPERATIVE SUSTAINED YIELD ACT*

*I wish E.T. Allen were here. The subject, as you know, that we are to discuss this morning was envisioned by E. T., a good many years ago, and I think it is peculiarly fitting that this Association should discuss this particular subject in view of his early interest in it and the efforts of that Association to make this sustained, this cooperative sustained yield idea possible.*

*Sixteen years ago–I think it was in the summer and fall of 1928–with financial encouragement by Charles Lathrop Pack, your Association organized and carried through a "Cooperative Forest*

*The Last Train on Lower Railroad Ave., Simpson Timber Co., Shelton April 7, 1948. Courtesy Simpson Timber Company*

Shelton-Mason County Journal

VOL. LX—NO. 51. SHELTON, WASHINGTON. Thursday, December 19, 1946. 6¢ PER COPY; $2.50 PER YEAR

# SIMPSON SUSTAINED UNIT CONTRACT SIGNED



Above is a map of the acreage which will be included in the sustained yield unit which will operate for the next 100 years, beginning Jan. 1, 1947, under a contract signed by the U. S. Government and the Simpson Logging Company last week and which includes forest lands owned by both the government and the company.

## REED, KREIENBAUM FORESEE PERMANENCY IN EMPLOYMENT HERE THROUGH 100-YEAR DEAL

## Government Announces Decision

Announcement of the execution of a contract between the Simpson Logging company and the United States government for the cooperative management of a huge tract of land in Mason, Eastern Grays Harbor and Thurston counties, for the next hundred years, was made in Washington, D. C., last Thursday morning.

Stability, for a full century, is the keynote of the cooperative sustained yield agreement just concluded. The company operates at Shelton and McCleary. For the first time in history, the conception of cooperative forest management by the government and its citizens, long dreamed of by forestry officials and sanctioned by Congress in public law 273 (March 29, 1944) is now realized.

The stability is tangible and real. A total of 159,000 acres of company lands are managed, for the 100 years, with 111,000 acres of National Forest under unified management for continuous production. Their yield is estimated at 90 to 100 million feet of timber every year; but thickening stocks on portions of the area should increase the annual harvest as time runs on. The entire cut will flow into the lumber, plywood, pulp, door, furniture and fibre board plants at Shelton and McCleary.

### Security for 100 Years

This agreement underwrites—for a century—the security of two forest home communities. It insures the jobs and payrolls of 1,375 workers at Simpson Logging camps and mills and the livelihood of the 4,000 people whom they support. More than that, it offers the loggers and mill employees the best opportunity for satisfactory working conditions, for good schools, family life and home ownership. Sustained yield under the Shelton plan stands at the opposite pole from the "...

*Study of the Grays' Harbor Area" and published the results of the study here in Portland in 1929. Many of those here today will remember this study for they actively participated in it. I recall very vividly my own part in the study and the field trips with E. T. Allen, Professor Alexander, Norman Jacobson, and others.*

*The basic thought behind this project of the Western Forestry and Conservation Association was this: Here in Grays' Harbor County is a large area of forest land and numerous communities–Hoquiam, Aberdeen, Montesano, and others–existing almost entirely through exploitation of that forest land. There is obvious danger of exhaustion of the basic forest resources on which these communities depend. What can be done to meet this problem intelligently before it gets beyond solution?...*

*The purpose of the Cooperative Sustained Yield Act is "to promote sustained-yield forest management in order thereby (a) to stabilize communities, forest industries, employment, and taxable forest wealth; (b) to assure a continuous and ample supply of forest products; and (c) to secure the benefits of forests in regulation of water supply and streamflow, prevention of soil erosion, amelioration of climate, and preservation of wildlife." The Act gives the Secretaries of Agriculture and Interior authority to establish cooperative sustained-yield units on lands under their respective jurisdiction, to enter into cooperative agreements for coordinated management of public and private timber, to establish sustained-yield units composed entirely of Federal lands, to enter into cooperative agreements that other Federal, State, or local public agencies, and within these sustained-yield units to sell government timber at its appraised value without competitive bidding.*

*Simpson Timber Company entered into the 100-year Shelton Cooperative Sustained Yield Unit with the Forest Service in 1946 under provisions of Public Law 273, enacted by Congress in 1944. The unique project was begun to provide a sustained timber supply and future crop through sound forest management practices in order to stabilize the economy of the lumber mill towns of Shelton and McCleary.*

The 1940's brought new concepts to timber management. Able foresters such as George Drake and Ed Hanzlik were able to realistically put into practice the basic precepts of Pinchot and Graves:

*In line with the primary objective of "the greatest good of the greatest number in the long run" the Forest Service applies two basic principles in the management of national-forest resources. One of these is the principle of "sustained yield". Sustained-yield management of timber means that the forest is managed for maximum continuous production of timber of desirable kinds. The techniques of sustained-yield management vary greatly with different forest types, but the objective is always the same-continous renewal of timber crops to replace those harvested. The sustained-yield principle applies not only to timber, but to forage grazed by livestock, to wildlife, and to other renewable resources... [sic]*

In a speech on forest programs to the Port Angeles Chamber of Commerce September 8, 1941, two months before Pearl Harbor, Olympic Forest Supervisor Carl B. Neal outlined the following points:

*You need to keep your forest land productive through better fire protection and through increased reforestation.*

*Research to promote more profitable utilization.*

*Research and federal loans to promote better markets for finished products.*

*State and Federal acquisition to control liquidation.*

*Public Regulation of Private Forest Practices.*

*Financial contribution in lieu of taxes.*

The Armed Forces used a greater tonnage of wood than of steel. Many peacetime activities were curtailed, such as the nationwide forest survey, reforestation work, and land acquisition. To help stimulate output of wood for war needs, a special Timber Production War Project was launched. This boosted lagging production and at the same time encouraged logging methods that left trees for future use and wasted as little as possible.

With so many men serving in the armed services, regular fire protection forces were severely depleted. In a memo which was forwarded to the Regional Office and the War Production Board in Portland, Oregon, Forester George Drake relates the urgency and concern related to the manpower shortage in 1943:

*One of the most distressing aspects of the whole problem is the fact that we are being handicapped all the time on the part of certain men in the crew as to being on the job. There is hardly a week that we do not lose the services of several men due to drunkenness over the week-end. With normal sized crews, this is not too serious, but with scant crews, the loss of a few chokermen or fallers cuts heavily into production and efficiency. This is a problem that as a company, we are unable to control in these times, where in normal times, these men would be discharged and replaced by men that would stay sober. It seems that, if the men themselves wish to make a real contribution to the war effort, they should take steps to remedy this problem themselves.*

*Like so many human enterprises, forest management began with fire management. In the United States, it was fire that had helped to create professional forestry and had directed the paths of cooperative forestry. Fire control advertised and dramatized forest conservation–and the Forest Service role–as no other public message could have done. Forestry had not brought fire protection; on the contrary, it was the need for fire control on the lands of the counter reclamation that often created the need for a technical bureau to oversee the protection of these lands, and it was professional forestry's good fortune to take charge of that bureau. That is, professional forestry in the United States developed in large measure not in spite of fire but because of it. The Forest Service survived in its early years because it learned to control fire; it has endured because, with time, it has learned to accommodate fire. The Service's greatest nemesis has, in many respects, been its greatest benefactor.*

*Stephen J. Pyne, "A Cultural History of Wildland and Rural Fire"*

The brief recorded history of the Olympic Peninsula begins with the first Spanish sighting of Santa Rosalia (now known as Mt. Olympus) by Juan Perez. He also observed in his log:

> *Smoke of forest fires shrouded the Washington Coast.*

Olympic Forest ecologists have noted:

> *The occurrence of wildfires on the Olympic Peninsula is closely tied to climate and climatic history. It appears that the pattern of fires has been as variable as the pattern of past climates. Some periods have had many stand destroying fires, others have had almost none. Still other periods may have had a pattern of high frequency but low fire intensity. Because of this variability and the many factors involved, one aspect of the fire history of the Olympics seems certain—one cannot characterize the fire patterns of one period by knowing what it is in another. Our earliest evidence of fire in the Olympics comes from a bog in the Hoh River drainage.*
>
> *Three great burning periods occurred from 1300 to 1750 during the Little Ice Age. Our knowledge of the fire history increases greatly about 1000 years ago. Prior to that time, we can only speculate about fires, based on evidence such as charcoal preserved in bogs and our knowledge of different tree species.*

*Roots of Western Hemlock Exposed by the Result of Fire. 1897 Photo by Gifford Pinchot, During His Inspection of Olympic Peninsula*

> *For the period of the past 1000 years, we can study living trees (Douglas-fir and western redcedar both live to over 1000 years) and refer to historical records to construct a much more detailed picture of the fire history. [sic]*

It is speculated that the large prairies at LaPush, Forks, Sequim, and Nisqually are the result of repeated fires. A brief summary of historical fires provides the background for the 1907 Sol Duc Burn which is vividly documented by Ranger Chris Morgenroth. A chronology of major historic fires is available at the Olympic National Forest Headquarters.

> *•Ludlow-Quilcene Fire—1864*
>
> *This fire burned about the close of the Civil War - roughly, 1864. Started in the slashing around Port Ludlow with a high east wind, and wound up on Mt. Walker - Mt. Turner, and the Quilcene Range. Although the fire evidently burned for weeks, most of the area was covered in one or two days, as remembered by old timers. [sic]*

*•Neilton/Quinault Burn—1885*

*Started from burning to clear right-of-way on old Quinault trail – went into crowns and crowned out about 2,000 acres. There have been a number of smaller fires in this locality. [sic]*

*The original survey of the Soleduck Valley in early 1890's show several burns, one of about 2,000 acres, covering the recent Kugel Creek thinning and running area. The ridge between Bear Creek and the Pysht River has had at least 2 burns. The first one left a few big Douglas-fir trees that evidently stood for many years and were killed by a later fire. A big fire on the south fork of the Pysht in the 70's or 80's was a roaring crown fire according to two trappers in the area at the time. This would tie in to the second burn of Bear Creek Ridge as to time judged by age classes, but the two burned did not join, as merchantable timber has been logged for several miles between. [sic]*

*•Dungeness Country—1890-91*

*Mr. Burroughs of Port Angeles recounts that fires burned in the foothills back of Sequim the Fall of 1890, covering large areas. Rainfall that winter was light and the fires never went out, smoldering in logs and duff all winter... [sic]*

*The Spring of 1891, the fires again took off on a wide front and burned all summer. By the time winter rains started, the entire Dungeness drainage was burned with the exception of a few pockets of timber. Mr. Burroughs recalls that the smoke was so heavy it was stifling a good part of the spring and summer – visibility was limited to about 100 feet. Peoples' eyes, nose, and throat were so irritated by the smoke that the eyes were red and watered constantly – most people had sore throats. The animals were likewise affected and were listless and no longer run from man. When Blue Mountain burned, the wind was so strong they barricaded the front door to keep it from blowing open and the roof from blowing off. They were in the orchard until about midnight; it was very warm, and at times large pieces of burning material fell in the clearing. Early tabulations show 30,000 acres of*

*Oscar Peterson Pack Train on Trail to Kloshe Nanich. Courtesy Peterson Family*

*old burns on the Quilcene district, largely in the Dungeness drainage. [sic]*

*The first records show that there was an old burn of 7000 acres on the Hamma Hamma, that had "burned before the days of organized protections" from the references, this day may have been one of the "91" or "02" burns. [sic]*

*Typical Burn Areas Near Snider*

*•Elma—Humptulips—1902*

*The fire burned in 1902 with the big run on September 11. Homesteaders in the Satsop Wynoochee country were hard put to save their homes - semi-gloom prevailed at noon, etc. The old story of "Dark Days" so common to everyone familiar with fire history and runs from Elma to Humptulips Railroad. [sic]*

*Early Burns and Reforestation Efforts on the Olympic, 1910 U.S. Forest Service photo by Chris Morgenroth*

The immediate damage that wildfire brought to the frontier is vividly portrayed in the account of the 1907 Sol Duc fire written by Chris Morgenroth in *Footprint of the Olympics*, edited by his daughter Katherine Flaherty. Excerpts are as follows:

*Planting Crew, December 1910, a Cold Morning. Courtesy Katherine Morgenroth Flaherty*

*Our first job was to keep the fire from reaching Lake Crescent. Settlers around the lake loaded axes, shovels, and mattocks. Theodore Rixon, who was on the Soleduck River with a railway survey crew, let us have eight more men. The wind was coming from the east so I urged the men to work fast to complete and hold the fire line, hoping that the wind would die down by evening. We were able to make a backfire line from the valley floor to the top of the ridge above the west end of the lake.*

*Cauliflower-shaped smoke clouds were billowing four to five hundred feet into the air. Burning tree limbs, five inches in diameter, were being sucked up into the hot air and exploding like skyrockets, spreading fire in every direction, the sight was awesome and terrifying, making me wonder if it would consume the whole countryside.*

*Frank Speak, Packer; Jos. Schulz, Helper; Re-planting the Sol Duc Burn, 1910. Courtesy Katherine Morgenroth Flaherty*

> *A pack train heading for the Sol Duc Hot Springs happened along with two boxes of stumping powder. We borrowed the powder, cut each stick into two cartridges and with a pole sharpened at one end we made holes eighteen inches deep and six feet apart. By setting the dynamite off, the thick mossy cover of humus was blasted off, exposing dirt and rock. This made an effective fire line and stopped the deep-seated ground fire. This was the first time dynamite was used to build a fire line.*

The final irony of the fire which started as a result of land-clearing on the Mueller Ranch, was that Chris paid the entire cost of fighting this fire from money received through his personal note at a Port Angeles Bank. The Forest Service did not have a fiscal agent closer than Washington, D.C., and it took nearly two years before he was reimbursed.

In a letter to J. Herbert Stone after his retirement, Ranger Bill Bryan reminisces:

> *Most of my memories of the 1924-30 period tie in with fires. I arrived at Quilcene about August, 1924 in time to see a fire, starting at Dry Creek on the upper end of the Penny Creek road, sweep to the top of Green Mountain. Neither Vallad or I had any previous firefighting experience. The fire reached a size of about 1700 acres. Most of the crew of about 150 men came from the Seattle "skid road", a common practice continuing up to the time of the CCC programs. Many of the crew were "slick-shod" misfits, but there were a few experienced fire fighters, and their advice in fire technique was a great help. In view of the present policy, it is hard to believe that Vallad and myself were the overhead. August 25 is a firm date. It*

*rained hard that day and resulted in the first real sleep either of us had for the three weeks... [sic]*

*In July, 1925, Snow Creek Logging Company celebrated the approaching end of their sale with a fire. It smouldered for several days before taking off through the Mt. Zion gap to the head of Deadfall Creek. Tom Talbott, R-6 law enforcement officer, was at Quilcene. Since the fire was beyond the sale boundary, he suggested district action. Gathering a crew of about fifteen "homeguards", we went up the Little Quilcene trail. The next day, "Doc" Billingsley and about thirty men arrived. The fire was checked on the south side of the Zion gap. A few days later, with the crew in camp for lunch, we were disturbed by a sudden down valley wind of considerable force and an unfamiliar noise from the slope below us. Because of dense smoke covering the valley for several days, visibility was limited to a few hundred feet. Charlie McClanahan went down to investigate and was back shortly with word that a crown fire was coming up the slope. [sic]*

*Throwing the tools in the creek, we headed for the Zion gap burn which had cooled to a point of reasonable safety as long as one didn't stand too long in the same spot. What happened was that the fire in Snow Creek had spread by way of Lord's Lake eastward along Green Mountain and west up the Little Quilcene in the matter of a few hours. I believe this was the first fire for the newly formed Regional Flying Squadron, a group of five or six experienced firemen who acted as overhead throughout the region. At any rate, there was help from other forests. This was also my first introduction to gravity hose lines. [sic]*

*Lightning fires at the head of Tunnel Creek in 1929 was the first time that a fire crew was supplied by aerial drop. A crew of about forty men were working out of a central camp on two fires in rugged country without trails. Included in the crew were Walter Lund and his party of cruisers, which also included Allen R. Cochran, recently retired from R-7. J.R. Bruckart, Assistant supervisor, arranged for two drops on successive days. Both canned and fresh supplies were packed in burlap sacks together with blankets to offer some protection. The sacks were stacked in a cabin plane with Robert McClay of the supervisor's staff acting as dropper, or perhaps bombardier is a better word. The fire camp was located in a small meadow near the edge of a shallow pond. On the first, the plane circled the camp to get a bearing. On the next circle, the plane door flew open and McClay started kicking out the sacks with his feet while holding on to the inside of the plane with his hands. The first two sacks out were filled with bread and both landed in the pond. Bruckart and I had stationed ourselves on a ridge a short distance from and about 200 feet above the camp to spot the fall of the sacks. One sack landed near us and canned corn flew like shrapnel. These were free drops from an altitude of about 300 feet above camp to 50 where the plane crossed the Tunnel Creek-Dosewallips divide. Supplies came through in surprisingly good shape. In all, about 60 sacks were dropped in the two days and all but one was recovered. The second drop included a copy of the Seattle Times with a vivid description of men surrounded by fire being supplied from the air. In the meantime, Frank Ritter, forest engineer, with a large crew were building a trail from near Corrigenda Guard Station to the ridge above the fire camp. This trail was built in about three days, and from then on, the camp was supplied by pack horses. [sic]*

The most dramatic and devastating fire to occur on the Olympic National Forest was the Port Angeles Western (PAW) fire. At the time Lew Evans was the protective assistant and Sanford Floe was the ranger at Snider. Lew received the fire report from the North Point Lookout. As east winds fanned the fire into an inferno which threatened the logging community of Forks, Ranger Floe observed:

*The saddest point of my career was at 6:00 A.M. on September 20, 1951, standing on the Kloshe Nanitch road watching the Forks fire roar down the North Fork Calawah.*

As a Forest Service wife living with her husband, Dick, at Snider Ranger Station, Nina Woodcock recalled her role during the Forks fire in an account in *Timberlines*, The Thirty-Year Club publication:

*1 SEPTEMBER 1951 — THE FORKS FIRE*

*By Nina Woodcock*

*It was 6:00 in the morning. It was my neighbor, Dorothy, saying, "There won't be any school today. Lew wouldn't let me call you before, but there's a big fire. It started at 4:30." I was too sleepy to be impressed. Another of those fires, I thought. Must be close to the highway or the school bus would be running. Dorothy was getting impatient.*

*"This is a big one. Take a look out your kitchen window!"*

*The sky was the smokey bronze of flame veiled by smoke. This was big. I rushed back to the phone, wide awake now. A 60 miles an hour wind was moving the fires so fast, nothing could stop it.*

*It had already burned 6 miles, skipping from one mountaintop to the next, creating its own downdrafts to fan the flame.*

*"No danger as yet." Dorothy said. "They'll get us out in plenty of time if it's necessary.."*

*My first thought was of Dick. He and Jim, Patty's husband, were camping out for the week.*

*We looked out the window at the front of the house to see flames roaring up the mountain about two miles away.*

*Just before noon, the men walked in the door, and ... they told us their story.*

*They saw a big cloud and decided that it might be a "smoke" in which case they'd be needed, it would be wise to come out. They hiked for miles out to the pickup truck and then followed an old logging road toward the highway. There wasn't room to turn around. The fire had just started here and the roads seemed clear, so they made a run for it. The next few minutes gave them enough excitement to last a lifetime.*

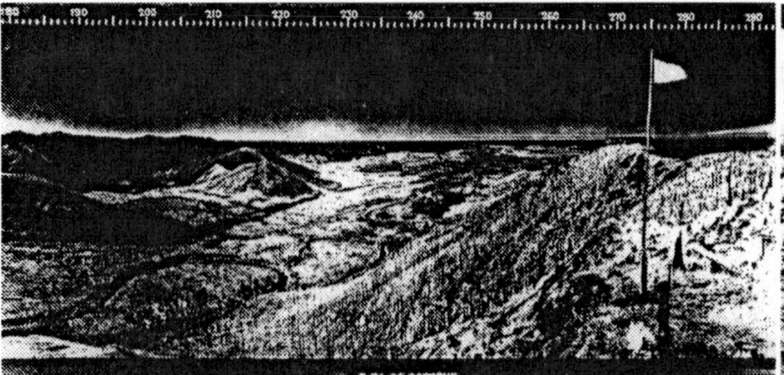

*As they were telling us about their narrow escape, Lew came with the latest news of the fire. It was still urged on by a strong wind and was expected to burn to the sea unless merciful rain came.*

*That night, I was asked to help with the timekeeping work that would begin the next morning when the hundreds of necessary fire fighters would start arriving.*

*The men were up till midnight talking fire and laying plans for fighting it. It was impossible to get to sleep that night.*

*The next day was just as hectic with men pouring in all day. Another camp was set up to alleviate the crowding. During the time of the fire, approximately 600 men came in, some from out of state.*

*The fourth day, the wind had changed. It was a breeze in our general direction and the smoke was as thick as heavy fog. By this time, the fire had crossed the highway 18 miles west of us and was burning its way towards the sea. It had burned an area 20 miles long and three to five miles wide. It was dark all day. We knew the sun was there somewhere beyond the smoke, but couldn't see it.*

*On the sixth day, the blessed rain came and contrary to custom, we welcomed it.*

In 1951, Kelly Coon was a young junior forester on the Skykomish District of the Snoqualmie National Forest. His recollections of the fire:

*I was called out for a fire on Donkey Creek at Quinault and hauled three other Snoqualmie folks (Bob Norton, Len Flower, and Jim Lowrie) to the fire in my 1941 Cadillac sedan. (We travelled pretty well in those days).*

*We were in a fire camp at Humptulips Guard Station for a day or so when we were called out of the evening chow line and reassigned to a fire that had broken out on the P.A. &W. Railroad near Snider. I hauled the same guys who'd come with me to Donkey Creek, plus Ross Files, another Snoqualmieite, to Snider. We got there fairly late, so we bedded down in one of the old tarpaper bunkhouse at Snider until about 4:00 AM.*

*We were assigned a Division on the west side of the fire and I supervised a catroad built down*

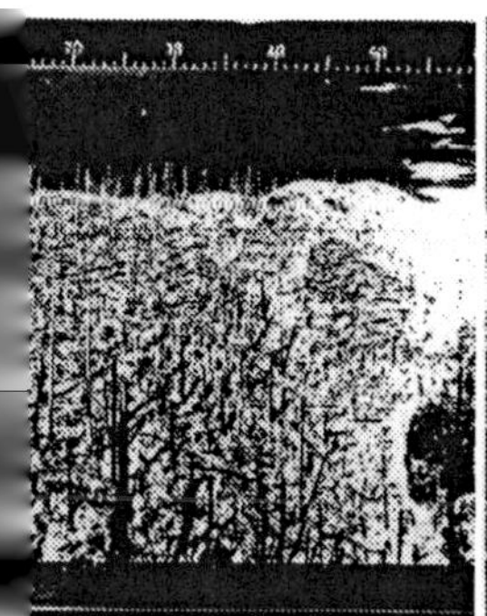

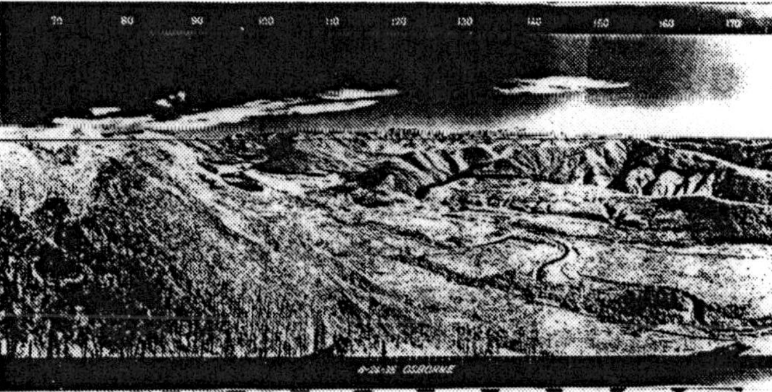

*The Forks Fire, September 1951. Photo by Lew Evans, District Assistant*

*Remains of Burned House, Outskirts of Forks, Sanford Keys and Dog*

*a ridge on the southwest side of the fire. A day or so later, the rains came and we went home. The fire was about 1500 acres and had originated from a rod bearing failure on a PAW steam locomotive. The fire was manned for mopup by pickup crews. This was in early July.*

*About 30 days later, I was called out again for the Forks Fire. Lo and behold, it started, I was told by Lew Evans at Snider, from a buried chunk in the catroad we'd built down the ridge on the west side of the PAW fire. I was sent up to the same place I'd been a month before with a crew from Mayr Brothers headed by a young logger named Werner Mayr, and we started west along the south flank of the fire. By this time, the fire had made its main run and was in the outskirts of Forks. It was fairly cool where we were so it was just the job of lining the edge. Mayr had a good crew and really worked them. [sic]*

The entire Olympic Peninsula was mobilized in a democratic spirit reminiscent of pioneer days, where community spirit and self-reliance merged. [Authors note]:

*This was made very real to me as a seventeen year old high school senior at Lake Quinault. Football had just been introduced in 1951 and five of us, including my brother, Jerry, were reluctantly given permission by Coach Cory, to leave school and the football practice field. We were hired as flunkies in the fire camp established on the Calawah River with Clarence Edgington, the Protective Assistant at Quinault, assigned as Camp Boss.*

*Our school bus carrying loggers from the Quinault area passed through walls of fire when we reached the Calawah River road. Fire camp was on the banks of the river and we five flunkies served the meals to the fire fighters on the fireline. I recall a chartered Greyhound bus arriving with a group of fire fighters assembled from the Seattle Skid Road. Some wore street shoes and light clothing until they were able to order work boots from the commissary tent. The interlude from school provided a chance to earn money for school clothes. A highlight was snaring three large salmon from the Calawah River to augment one evening meal. Little did I realize that my first fire camp was to be my summer home two years later as fireguard and lookout for the Snider Ranger District.*

The wind changed, but not before Forks had been evacuated, Highway 101 closed and as reported by the September 27, 1951, edition of the *Forks Forum*:

*23 homes, 9 cabins, 3 barns, 4 garages, 1 sawmill, 4 railroad bridges, 1 mile of track and 40,000 acres were burned and blackened.*

*Various equipment and property not in the preceding list was also lost. One logging company lost two donkeys and other equipment as well as a stockpile of logs. Damage estimates a week after the fire went over six million dollars.*

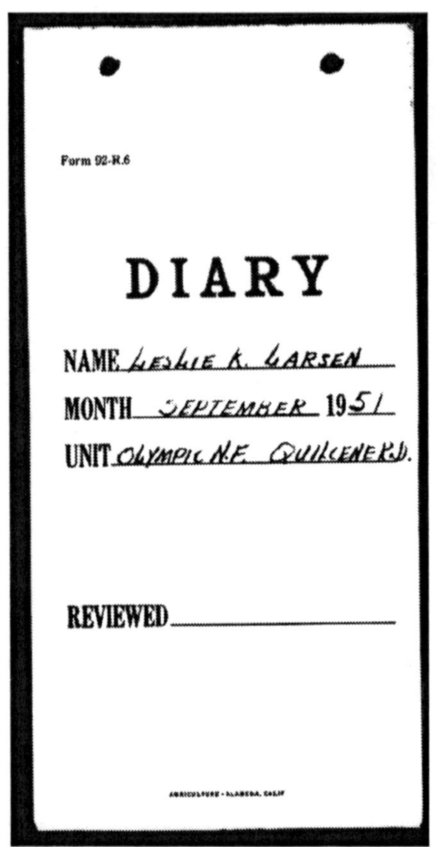

Form 92-R.6

DIARY

NAME Leslie K. Larsen

MONTH September 1951

UNIT Olympic N.F. Quilcene R.D.

REVIEWED

AGRICULTURE - ALAMEDA, CALIF

UNITED STATES
DEPARTMENT OF AGRICULTURE
FOREST SERVICE

EXPENSES

Speedometer readings personally owned car { Start / End — Miles

Other (itemize)

Major Functions

| | N.F. | P.J. | Total |
|---|---|---|---|
| 101.3 | | | 8 |
| 3/10a P.A.W. Fire | | | 4 |

6:10 a.m. Wheeler called from Olympia saying that Sandy's fire had blown up again & that Jay & I might have to go to the fire. He also wanted to know where Jack Ferrell was - told him Ferrell was here - we are to get handy-talkies ready to go to Snider.

Date September 20, 1951

Lew Evans confided that as a result of the blow-up of the Port Angeles Western Fire, his Forest Service diaries (as well as Ranger Floes') for January-September 1951, were confiscated as evidence in a suit filed against the government. Lew's counterpart at Quilcene, Les Larsen, kept meticulous records during his Forest Service career. His entries for 20-22 September, which have been preserved, illustrate the immediate concern on the Olympic.

> *6:10 a.m. — Wheeler called from Olympia saying that Sandy's fire had blown up again and that Jay and I might have to go the fire. He also wanted to know where Jack Ferrell was - told him Ferrell was here - we are to get handy - talkies ready to go to Snider.*

The law suit originally was won by the Forest Service but later overturned on appeal. The expert witness for the Olympic National Forest was George Lincoln Drake whose expertise was recognized by everyone in forestry.

*Forks Fire, 1951*

*Fire Dispatch, Les Larsen*

Supervisor Neal quickly mobilized salvage and rehabilitation efforts by suspending sales in the Quilcene and Quinault ranger districts. This prompt action enabled foresters to plan for the recovery operations of the approximately 500 million board feet lying within the burn area.

It was "round logs on flat cars" and Ranger Sanford Floe, once described as "a tough little Scot" was the right man to do it. The Port Angeles newspaper, in its issue of November 13, 1954, reported:

*COMPLETION BY SPRING*

*Sanford M. Floe, Olympic National Forest Soleduck District Ranger, said it hoped to have the salvage work completed by next Spring. "Then will come the longer forest rebuilding work," he said.*

*Loggers are working fast to get the damaged timber out to prevent a complete loss, Floe reported. Commercial loggers suspended operations in other areas and moved their equipment into the burn.*

*"You can't dally with burned timber, sap rot sets in and the ambrosia beetle comes along and bores into the heart of the tree. Blue stain, a fungus, gets into the holes, and then the flathead borer goes to work. First thing you know, you've got nothing," Floe said.*

*The district ranger handled the sales of the salvage timber and more than 40 logging companies are working in the burn. Many small gypo outfits are also in the area under subcontracts.*

*"The murderous thing about insects in a burn is not just the destruction of damaged timber," Floe explained. "A green tree protects itself by drowning insects with pitch or sap. A burned tree has very little or no sap."*

*Helicopter Seeding the Forks Burn, 1952. Photo by Lew Evans*

> *"When insects find a favorable condition - as in a burn - they thrive and multiply. They chew their way through a burn like a wave, getting stronger and more numerous. Then they move into adjoining green timber and by weight of numbers can devastate a forest that can normally fight off infestation..."*
>
> *"That's why you've got to move burned timber," Floe said. E.C. DeGraff, assistant Olympic National Forest Supervisor, said "They (the loggers) are getting almost complete utilization of damaged timber, down to 10 and 12-inch hemlock that loggers couldn't have bothered with a few years ago."*

Following the removal of the fire-killed timber from the Port Angeles Western conflagration, the monumental task of rejuvenating the forest land was thrust upon Ranger Sanford Floe. This goal of reforesting was accomplished in the autumn of 1958. The old-time maverick ranger had earned the respect of everyone in Clallam County and beyond. Lew Evans who worked for Ranger Floe since before WWII and knew him well, described an incident which typifies the dedication of this crusty woods veteran:

> *One time there was a problem with striking loggers who had fell a tree across one of the forest logging roads and wouldn't allow anyone to pass. Sandy, he strapped on his holster, jumped in his pickup and backed those people down; Sandy told them it was government land and everybody had access to entry. [sic]*

*Snow Creek, Quilcene Ranger District, Tree Planters Breaking Camp, 1929*

Ranger Floe's achievements and outstanding career culminated with the Superior Service award issued by the Department of Agriculture in 1957.

Beginning with the 1907 SolDuc fire, the Olympic National Forest has been directly involved and concerned in innovative and noteworthy accomplishments in reforestation. Excerpts from a memorandum by Julius F. Kummel, Forest Examiner, dated February 18, 1927, reveal a more sophisticated approach to regenerating a burn:

*With Ranger W.D. Bryan, the writer examined in June, 1926 that part of Snow Creek cut-over area burned in the fires of 1924 with the view of determining the portion in need of planting. The areas looked over are located in Secs. 32 and 33, T.27N., R.2W. and Secs. 4, 5, 6, 7, 8, 9, 17, T.28., R.2W. Roughly, the area cut over and burned totals 3500 acres. Approximately, also, 1750 acres of this were burned over in the fire of 1924 only, 1250 acres in both the fires on 1924 and 1925, and 500 acres in the 1925 fire only. Of the total cut-over and burned area of 3500 acres, approximately 1442 acres are recommended for planting.*

*Topographically, the area may be divided into two rather distinct units. The northern portion lying mainly in the Townsend Creek drainage and in the drainage of the creek flowing to the north, is characterized foremost part by gentle road slopes, except in the immediate vicinity of Townsend Creek where the slopes become quite steep. In the southern portion, the area is more broken up by Snow, Townsend, and Rixon Creeks and their tributaries, and by numerous knolls. Between Snow and Townsend Creeks there is quite a broad stretch of gently sloping area, but elsewhere in this southern portion, the topography is very rough with steep slopes predominating... [sic]*

*The area is readily accessible by trail from Crocker Lake on the Olympic Highway, from which point the eastern boundary of the area is about 4 miles distant. Numerous railroad grades reach to all portions of it. Construction of a road in from Blyn, 8 to 10 miles distant, utilizing the old mainline logging grade, is contemplated.*

*The fire hazard is much lower than on most planting projects because of the small number of tall snags and comparatively small amount of material on the ground on the portions considered for planting. Logging operations on the area are completed. A guard is stationed there during the fire season and the area is closed to recreational use during the danger season. When the road to Blyn is completed, the area will still have better protection...*

*The following supplemental report may be of interest in connection with the planting job designated above. I have rounded off cost figures to the nearest dollar.*

*SUPPLEMENTAL RECORD*

*The crew consisted of:*

- *1 Foreman @ $115.00 per month and board*
- *1 Foreman @ $110.00 per month and board*
- *1 Cook @ $110.00 per month and board*
- *1 Bull cook @ $ 75.00 per month and board*
- *1 Flunky @ $ 65.00 per month and board*
- *20-22 Planters @ $4.25 per day. $1.00 per day for board and a small fee for blanket laundry.*
- *1 Packer paid $4.00 per day and board and $2.00 per day for each pack horse used.*

*Ranger J. D. Ahl Scaling Logs, 1924*

*Planters were used as necessary to cut wood, drive truck and stake rows, and help with survey.*

*Assistant Supervisor Bruckart acted as superintendent and was assisted by Ranger Bryan and myself part time...*

Excerpts from a memorandum by R.D. Maclay, Junior Forester, April 28, 1927.

*Dennie Ahl Seed Orchard*

> *The first commercial thinning in a Douglas-fir plantation of the Northwest was conducted as a joint research project by the Olympic National Forest and the Experiment Station in the spring of 1951. The experimental thinning was confined to a five-acre area within the 1,500 acre Snow Creek plantations, established in 1927 adjacent to the old Snow Creek Guard Station...Three 1/2-acre permanent sample plots were installed after the thinning had been completed—2 plots in the thinned areas and one check plot in the unthinned stand... Report by Elmer W. Show, Forester, Pacific Northwest Forest and Range Experiment Station, June 20, 1952. [sic]*

The evolution of the Snow Creek plantations continues and is thriving to this day. However, it was not unique. Cooperative forestry projects were undertaken with private industry, such as the Olympia Airport forest which was documented in a formal report to Olympia City Commissioner Tom Evans. Another notable cooperative effort was the McCleary Experimental Forest project. Practical forestry had, indeed, come of age on the Olympic. Perhaps this is best illustrated by the inception of the Denny Ahl Seed Orchard:

> *In the fall of 1957, the Olympic National Forest established the first clonal seed orchard in the entire Forest Service system. The orchard was designed to produce frequent, abundant, and easily harvested crops of genetically improved tree seed from known superior parent trees. John D. "Dennie" Ahl worked for may years as a scaler on the Olympic National Forest. Ahl*

*lived in Eldon, Washington and scaled logs along the Hood Canal until his death in 1944. During the summer of that year, he suffered a fatal heart attack while rowing a boat across Lake Cushman. Ahl and a fire fighting crew had just controlled a lightning fire. Shortly after his death, a local fire lookout tower was named in his honor. In 1957, Ahl's name was bestowed on the seed orchard to honor his illustrious years of public service.*

In a letter dated October 19, 1989, John A. Pitcher, Director, Hardwood Research Council, Memphis, Tennessee., shared his experiences in the establishment of the orchard:

*The Call. It was in my senior year at the College of Forestry in upstate New York, when early one spring day in 1957, I was called to Prof. Friedrich Kalehn's office and introduced to Mason Bruce, then Supervisor of the Olympic National Forest. It seems that Mr. Bruce was on a recruiting trip (they did those things back in the mid-'50's). One of the items on his shopping list was finding a forester with some training in the brand new field of tree improvement.*

*That's where I came in, because I had taken Prof. Klaehn's basic tree improvement course in the fall semester and was at the time doing some special studies under his tutelage. Mr. Bruce offered me a job on the Olympic National Forest on the Shelton District with the understanding that one of my responsibilities would be to develop a grafted seed orchard for Douglas-fir. Prof. Klaehn encouraged me to accept. My wife was pregnant and the grandparents-to-be were less than enthusiastic when they discovered that my first job in forestry was to be 3,000 miles away on the opposite coast of the United States.*

*Getting started. When we arrived in Shelton in June of 1957, Bill and Sara Bryan made us welcome, along with Pat and Libby Hanna, Sam and Alice Poirer, Bob and Iris Steinhoff, Dehn and Ginny Welch, Eldon and Jean Manthey, Mrs. Mack, and Dick Chase. As the new JF on the District, I got a lot of variety in the first few months I was there. By fall, after an extended fire season that included a 3 week stint at Anderson Butte LO, I was ready to start on the seed orchard. Tom Greathouse was on the Timber Staff in Olympia and became a frequent visitor as we developed the plans for the orchard. A cut-over flat on the south side of Dennie Ahl LO was what we finally settled on for the seed orchard site. Several big old seed trees were removed in a timber sale. It was about this time, in the fall of '57, that Virgil Allen joined the Dennie Ahl seed orchard project, having been lured away from the apple orchards on the east side. That was a lucky move for the project since Virgil stayed with it for 30 years.*

*Laying out the area. The area was greatly overstocked with an abundance of both planted seedlings and natural reproduction. The plan was to use these seedlings as rootstock for field grafting. El Elerding helped with the layout and marking the rootstocks.*

*Once the seedlings were marked, the next step was to remove the other seedlings left on the nearly 10 acres of the seed orchard. We got a lot of them removed by making a Christmas tree sale. The rest, we had to cut and drag out to brush piles for burning. I remember Ed Laney was the crew boss on the job. We worked long, hard, and steady at cleaning out everything but the seedlings to be grafted.*

Virgil Allen

*Second orchard needed. About the time we completed the cutting of the seedlings on the orchard, we learned that the Snoqualmie NF wanted in, too. So, we set about to create a second orchard, using the skills we had learned in marking the first orchard. It was located behind the first orchard, separated from it by a low area of natural drainage. By that time, Elerding and Laney knew exactly what was needed so I was free to collect scions for grafting.*

*Results. We accomplished the entire project, grafting some 4,800 rootstocks in a matter of weeks under some rather strenuous field conditions. Initial results were amazing with nearly every rootstock having one or more scions showing active growth. Severe graft incompatibilities became evident in later years and many clones were eliminated from the orchard because of this phenomenon.*

Following Mr. Pitcher's departure to return to upstate New York, Virgil Allen was the man who made it happen. He seemed to coax the secrets from the seed. Under Virgil's guidance, the seed orchard was nurtured from its humble, local beginnings to a productive, nationally, and internationally recognized reforestation facility. Virgil's loyal dedication was rewarded with the Superior Service Award in 1979 for his contributions to intensive forest management. Visitors to the Denny Ahl Seed Orchard will pass by the Virgil E. Allen tree grove, a living memorial to his genius as the first person to successfully graft Douglas-fir trees and for being the inspiration behind the first Douglas-fir producing seed orchard in the world.

*I went to the woods because I wished to live deliberately, to front only the essential facts of life, and see if I could not learn what it had to teach, and not, when I came to die, discover that I had not lived.*

*Henry David Thoreau, "Walden"*

After the Second World War, working circles of planned timber sales became a reality for each of the ranger districts. Technology changes included mechanization and use of organized fire suppression crews. The trail crews, slash burning operations and smokechasers continued to use hand tools such as the crosscut saw, the peavy, the double-bitted axe until the late 1950s. The first chain saws were large and cumbersome and considered to be unsafe. The lookout system continued to function as positive components of the fire prevention program. In 1953, a "Trapper Nelson" backpack was the main arsenal of smoke chasers on the Olympic. It was found in certain lookouts where the firewatcher was expected to "chase" the smoke and also on the Dodge Power Wagons used by fire guards on suppression/patrol. The smoke chasers pack contained a pulaski fire tool (named after the famous ranger who led his crew to safety during the 1910 Idaho conflagration). A shovel with a removable handle, "C" rations (World War II food packets), a "bastard" file, and whetstone for sharpening were critical components as well. A map case containing map, compass, protractor, mirror for signaling, pencils and a Forest Service notebook was standard equipment. A sleeping bag (or wool blankets) was included as a smoke chaser was expected to find the smoke, contain the fire by constructing a fire line around it, and stay with the fire until it was out.

The wartime years marked the ending of an era with the retirement of Rudo Fromme on the Mt. Baker National Forest in 1943. The war in Europe turned in favor of the allies and Ranger Ralph Hilligoss left the outfit. The longtime administrative assistant, Clarence Adams, relinquished his pen but not until he had compiled historical data which provided so many facts and clues to this forest history. In 1946, that gentle giant of a man, Quinault Ranger Joe Fulton, left the Olympic and immediately hired on as fire warden for Simpson Timber Company. Carl B. Neal was the last Olympic National Forest person to be a direct link to Gifford Pinchot himself. Supervisor Neal was able, in 1953, to derive great satisfaction from the efficient and professional manner in which his Olympic staff had surmounted the logistics (and politics) of removal of the timber from the Forks fire, thus providing a fitting conclusion to his distinguished forty-three-year career. It was a time of great change in the Olympic National Forest. The editorial in the *Aberdeen World* for February 5, 1953, gives dimension to these changes:

*CARL NEAL TO RETIRE*

*Although he has earned and certainly is entitled to some years of leisure, Grays harbor will miss Carl B. Neal, Olympic National Forest supervisor, when he retires from service at the end of February.*

*At Ease Beside the Cool Lake Waters Within the Olympic National Forest. Photo by Asahel Curtis, Courtesy Washington State Historical Society*

*Neal has spent 40 years in public service, since 1939 as supervisor of the Olympic national forest, this region's great wood reservoir. His administration, we have always felt, has been extremely honest and fair, and so progressive and sound that the Olympic forest, one of the nation's largest, has been one of the country's best managed. [sic]*

*Neal's job has grown with the years, particularly since heavy timber sales and cutting began with the large block sales to Shelton and Grays Harbor loggers. The volume of timber cut in the Olympic national forest has almost doubled since Mr. Neal took over as supervisor. In recent years, there has been an increasing number of small operators working in the national forest, placing*

*Campers at Lake Quinault, 1927*

*a heavy burden upon administration, what with selection of timber sites for sale, roads, market conditions, cutting supervision, reforestation and the multitude of other problems entailed.*

*Mr. Neal has been cooperative with loggers and timber purchasers and especially with the communities which rely upon national forest timber to tide them over the virgin forest-new growth gap.*

*Grays Harbor appreciates the years of interest Mr. Neal has shown in behalf of its problems. He has been a good friend in court. We especially appreciate his work in connection with formation of our community working circle and his constant attention to our needs and aspirations.*

*The Oxbow Trestle, 190 Feet Above the Wynoochee River, Under Construction in 1939 Using 250,000 Board Feet of Timber. A Kinsey Photograph Courtesy of Simpson Timber Company*

*We will miss him for his work, but more so for his smile, his jovial spirit, his friendliness. Carl B. Neal is a man Grays Harbor always welcomed, largely because he was Carl Neal.*

*Carl says he doesn't know yet what he will do with his "spare time" after retirement. He owns his home in Olympia. He may stay there. However, it's a bet he will not wander far from the Northwest. Although a native of Nebraska, Carl has spent since 1913 in Oregon and Washington, and would be lost without trees all around. [sic]*

Sanford Floe was the last of the "mustang" rangers who hadn't felt the need for a ranger to go to college. In 1953 and 1954, he was respectfully called "Mister" Floe or "the Ranger" by the summer crews. Bill Bryan joined his colleagues on the retiree list in 1960, the year after Sanford Floe completed his federal career. The cadre of old-timers was officially history.

The atomic age irrevocably changed the world for all time. Yet, as late as 1955, the Olympic National Forest was seldom visited except by intrepid outdoorsmen who were also practical woodsmen.

The post-war years marked the attempt to return to normalcy in a weary, tumultuous world

*Indian Basketweaver on the Beach at Port Townsend. Courtesy Bert Kellogg*

nearly undone by mans' own efforts. Economic growth, escalated by the populationboom, resulted in a strident demand for housing and consumer goods. The welcome return of the automobile to the American scene stimulated travel and necessitated more efficient and numerous transportation routes to recreation areas. The Olympic National Forest adapted to the newly-mobile public and its demand for additional campgrounds and modern recreational facilities. The entry into the jet age also contributed to the expansion of tourism and severely impacted visitor use of existing recreational opportunities.

For the Forest Service, the Multiple-use Act of 1960 was to be the catalyst of change in response to the vigorous challenges confronting American society. Many of those, then vital, fundamental, social and environmental issues and decisions, remain to be reckoned with today.

*In 1960, the Olympic National Forest and Simpson Timber Company Co-operated with MGM Studios in the Filming of the Movie "Ring of Fire." The Film Scene Included the Spectacular "Spilling" of a Locomotive, Tender, and Two Coaches and the Destruction of the Abandoned Trestle. Courtesy of Simpson Timber Company*

Various motives may have inspired people to live on the Olympic Peninsula in the past: A homestead hacked out of the forest, religious freedom, refuge, or sanctuary from another place more confining, greed and profit from the abundant natural resources. The last vision of the American frontier was glimpsed by Gifford Pinchot and his early-day rangers in their efforts to bring order to the newly created federal forest on the peninsula. As stewards and custodians of the public trust, they had to contend with the very forces which were so vital to the frontier: rugged individualism, a scorn for an older society and a fundamental love for freedom.

*Interrorem Ranger's Cabin Under Construction During May 1907. Photograph by Emery J. Finch, Who Married Maybelle Peterson in 1908 and Resided With Her in the Cabin. Copy Courtesy Jack Grubb*

*The Elwha Post Office During the Early Twentieth Century. It Operated From a Roofed Hollow Tree Stump Until 1926. Courtesy Bert Kellogg*

Aldo Leopold, that great original thinker, environmental advocate, and forest ranger, eloquently lamented the situation in a philosophical perspective in *A Sand County Almanac*:

*Man always kills the thing he loves, and so we the pioneers have killed our wilderness. Some say we had to. Be that as it may, I am glad I shall never be young without wild country to be young in. Of what avail are forty freedoms without a blank spot on the map?*

The pioneer destroys the very thing he loves the most...the wilderness. Yet, in a strange paradox, man has preserved his frontier heritage by setting aside forested areas where he may find physical solitude or a special renascence of the human spirit. Others pursue the eternal quest for new frontiers, seeking in the corridors of space and time a wilderness of the mind.

*An 18 Foot Cedar Between the Hoh and Clearwater, 1908. Photo by Chris Morgenroth*

## SUGGESTED READINGS AND BIBLIOGRAPHY

Alcorn, R. L. and G. D. 1966. *The Higley's, Lake Quinault Pioneers.* Aberdeen Daily World, 27 January to 5 March 1966, Aberdeen, Washington

Campbell, Patricia. 1977. *A History of the North Olympic Peninsula.* The Daily News, Port Angeles, Washington

Carpenter, Cecelia Smith. 1977. *They Walked Before, the Indians of Washington State.* The Washington State American Revolution Bicentennial Commission, Tacoma, Washington. 71 p.

Clelland, Lucille Hor. 1973. *Trails and Trials of the Pioneers of the Olympic Peninsula, State of Washington.* Humptulips Pioneer Association, Aberdeen, Washington

Dodwell, Arthur, and T. F. Rixon. 1902. *Forest Conditions in the Olympic Forest Reserve, Washington.* U.S. Geological Survey Professional Paper, Series H, 7(4):1-21.

Dooley, Clara Knack. "My Queets Story." Unpublished. Photocopy. 1965 (Available at Timberland Regional Library, Aberdeen, Washington.)

Evans, Gail E. H. 1983. *Historic Resource Study, Olympic National Park.*

Fish, Harriet. 1983. *Tracks, Trails and Tales;* 1979. *What's Down that Road*; 1978. *Fish Tales of Lake Crescent*

Gilman, S. C. 1896. *The Olympic Country.* The National Geographic Magazine 7(4): 133-139.

Gunther, Erna. 1972. *Indian Life on the Northwest Coast of North America as Seen by the Early Explorers and Fur Traders During the Last Decade of the Eighteenth Century.* The University of Chicago Press, Chicago IL, 262 p.

Gunther, Erna. 1973. *Ethnobotany of Western Washington.* Revised edition [1945]. University of Washington Press, Seattle, Washington.

Hoonan, Charles E. 1964. *Neah Bay, Washington: A Brief Historical Sketch*, Crown Zellerbach Corporation.

Hult, Ruby. [1954]. *The Untamed Olympics: The Story of a Peninsula.* Portland, Oregon: Binfords and Mort. Reprint 1971.

---------. 1975. *Herb Crisler in the Olympic Mountain Wilds, 1918-1951.* Ca. Ventura, California: Crisler-Hult-McAndrew. 1975.

James, Dave. 1986. *Grisdale, Last of the Logging Camps.* Mason County Historical Society.

Jefferson County Historical Society. 1966. *With Pride in Heritage: a History of Jefferson County, a Symposium*. First edition. Professional Publishing Printing Inc., Port Townsend, Washington.

Keatts, Robert. *Mining on the North Fork Skokomish River.* 1982. Belfair, Washington: Mason County Historical Society.

Kirk, Ruth. 1964. *Exploring the Olympic Peninsula*, University of Washington Press, Seattle, Washington.

Kirk, Ruth. 1966. *Olympic Rain Forest*. University of Washington Press, Seattle, Washington.

Kresak, Ray. 1984. *Fire Lookouts of the Northwest*. Ye Galleon Press, Spokane, Washington.

Lofgren, Svante E. *Barth ar-kell: (The White Bear).* Seattle: 1949 Publications Press.

Marston, Elizabeth. *Rain Forest*. Boston: Branden Press. 1969.

Meany, Edmund S. 1957. *Vancouver's Discovery of Puget Sound*. Binford and Mort, Portland, OR.

Morgan, Murray. 1955. *The Last Wilderness*. Viking Press, New York, New York.

Morganroth, Chris. 1991. *Footprints in the Olympics: An Autobiography*. Edited by Katherine Morganroth Flaherty, Ye Galleon Press.

Olson, Ronald L. 1936. *The Quinault Indians*. University of Washington Publications in Anthropology 6(1):1-185.

Pinchot, Gifford. 1947. *Breaking New Ground*. Originally published by Harcourt, Brace and Co., New York, NY.

Pyne, Stephen J. 1982. *Fire In America*. Princeton University Press.

Ruby, Robert, and John Brown. 1976. *Myron Eells and the Puget Sound Indians*. Superior Publishing Company, Seattle, Washington, 122 p.

Russell, Jervis, Editor. 1971. *Jimmy Come Lately; History of Clallam County*. Clallam County Historical Society, Port Angeles Washington.

Smith, Leroy. 1976. *Pioneers of the Olympic Peninsula*. Olympic Graphic Arts, Inc., Forks, Washington, 109 p.

Spring, Ira and Fish Byron. 1981. *Firewatchers Lookouts of the Olympics and Cascades*, Seattle Mountaineers.

Steen, Harold K. 1976. *The U.S. Forest Service. A History*. University of Washington Press.

Swan, James G. 1872. *The Northwest Coast; or Three Year's Residence in Washington Territory*. [New York, 1857.] Paperback Edition, University of Washington Press, Seattle, Washington.

Taylor, Eva Cook. 1972. *The Lure of Tubal Cain*. Jefferson County Historical Society, Port Townsend, Washington.

Thomas, Berwyn B. 1985. *Shelton, Washington. The First Century, 1885-1985*.

Turner, Frederick Jackson. 1920. *The Frontier in American History*. Henry Holt and Company Inc.,

Van Syckle, Edwin. *The River Pioneers: Early days on Grays Harbor*, ed. 1982. David James. Seattle: Pacific Search Press and Friends of the Aberdeen Public Library.

Van Syckle, Edwin. 1980. *They Tried to Cut it All*. Friends of the Aberdeen Public Library

Webster, E. B. *The King of the Olympics*. 1920. Port Angeles, Washington.

Weinstein, Robert. 1978. *Grays Harbor. 1885-1913*. Penguin.

Wood, Robert L. 1976. *Across the Olympic Mountains: The Press Expedition, 1889-90*. The Mountaineers and the University of Washington Press, Seattle, Washington, 197 p.

Wood, Robert L. 1976. *Men, Mules, and Mountains—Lieutenant O'Neill's Olympic Expeditions*. The Mountaineers, Seattle, Washington.

*Permission to quote from the following sources is gratefully acknowledged:*

*The excerpt from* BREAKING NEW GROUND *by Gifford Pinchot, courtesy of The Estate of Gifford Pinchot. Published by Harcourt Brace and Company (1947).*

*The quoted material by Melville Bell Grosvenor and the April 1896 cover courtesy of* NATIONAL GEOGRAPHIC MAGAZINE.

*The paragraph from* FIRE IN AMERICA *by Stephen J. Pyne. 1982 Princeton University Press.*

*The excerpts from* THE FRONTIER IN AMERICAN HISTORY *originally published by Henry Holt and Company, 1920.*

*The quotation from* A SAND COUNTY ALMANAC *by Aldo Leopold, courtesy Oxford University Press, Galaxie Book Edition, 1970.*

Jack Rooney has made an indelible contribution to documenting the history of the Olympic National Forest. Typical of Jack, he attributed the completion of Frontier Legacy to the many other thoughtful women and men who took photographs, contributed documentation, or simply cared and saved important maps and artifacts.

Jack's contribution, however, is especially noteworthy. Frontier Legacy was a major endeavor that took over five years to complete, as Jack would seasonally retreat to his retirement home in Mexico.

Jack accomplished a great deal since that first draft, although logistics, progress, and details seemed insurmountable at times.

We will be forever grateful for his contribution and are deeply indebted.

T. I. 'Dutch' Notenboom
Heritage Program Manager / Editor
Olympic National Forest

Printed in the United States
200776BV00002B/1-51/A

9 780914 019589